THE RIGHT TO MONEY

Book 8
in
Magic Q&A Book Series

KSENIA MENSHIKOVA

More about the Menshikova School:

Copyright © 2024 Ksenia Menshikova
English Translation Copyright © 2024
STUDIO LABYRINTH Sp. z o.o., Poland
All rights reserved.
ISBN: 9798321760581

CONTENTS

Introduction..	4
THE RIGHT TO MONEY...	7
THE CASTE SYSTEM OF THIS WORLD....................	71
Afterword..	170
Addendum 1 THE CHANNELS OF PHOEBUS AND DIONYSUS..	171
Addendum 2 GEIS..	210

INTRODUCTION

Magic is infinite. It's everywhere. It's in everything. The more you get to know it, the greater it becomes - in understanding, in sensations, in questions. We search for answers, we create new ones, and it will always be this way as long as there is magic.

We have chosen the path of infinite knowledge because we cannot do otherwise. With each answer we find, one of the millions of barriers standing between a person and magic disappears. Every day we understand something new, and through this understanding we become more and more connected to the world created by magic.

We study nature and gods, natural sciences, and history; we understand the past and see the future. We see this world as the currents of information processes and energy connections, we learn to distinguish patterns and sense uncertainties. We learn.

To make learning interesting and effective, the School was created at some point of time. There are five Departments in the Menshikova School (SMK), and everyone can unlock their own magic in the way they personally see fit.

For you to be able to ask your questions, the "MAGIC UNITED" forum was created, this is where discussions take place about everything that is important to you and everything you are searching for.

To ensure that the knowledge gathered by all of us does not go to waste, we wrote these books.

We— the founder of Menshikova's school, the teachers, and its students— are united: young mages and those who have just embarked on this path, those who are contemplating or have already decided. Together, we practice magic in this reality.

This is the eighth book in the "Magic in Questions and Answers" series, and there will be many more. Each one is dedicated to a specific topic but reflects many facets of hundreds of other topics that have yet to be uncovered. We wrote this together—students and teachers—on the "MAGIC UNITED" forum, during our personal meetings, and in open discussions. We continue writing because knowledge is the most valuable thing we have, and freedom of thought is what we will have. And also, because books should be read, not burned. And because we need magic—like air, like water, like fire, like earth, like life, like everything.

The previous book was about runes and the rules for entering them. We discussed the possibility of combining magic and religion, and how to transition from Christianity to paganism. We also covered the topic of egregores and explored how to break free from their influence.

In this book:
- *We will talk about the right to money.*

• We will discover why some people are always wealthy, while others are perpetually in debt.
• We will discuss the caste system.
• And explore whether a person can change their position within the social structure of society.

We write our books together. Join us.
Respectfully, *Menshikova*, mentors and students of the SMK.

THE RIGHT TO MONEY

How can you tell if you have the right to money or not? Why do some people seem to create money out of thin air, while others can never escape debt and loans? Is there any predestination involved in this?

The right to money is not just a metaphor—it's a very real and powerful program of the mind. However, it's important to note that this is not purely a psychological aspect, and this right cannot simply be acquired through commercial education or upbringing. The right to money runs much deeper and is rooted primarily in a correct understanding of oneself.

The thing is, many people today live under certain illusions regarding their personal identity. On one hand, this is good: the absence of caste-based burdens, social norms, and restrictions on one's rights and possibilities opens up prospects for personal growth. This kind of freedom is beneficial for many. But there is also another side. If we honestly face it, we'll see that this seemingly open path is fraught with hidden dangers, the most significant of which is a misjudgment of one's starting position in life.

Let me explain with a simple example involving bank loans. There are two categories of people who take out loans. The first group consists of people who, upon receiving something on credit, put it to work. An entrepreneur or businessman understands that a loan is only justified if every borrowed penny generates, say, twenty extra pennies in return. They know part of that will go back to the lender, but the rest contributes to a growing program for future success. What will they spend it on? Only things that will bring in more money, leading to further profits. Will they use borrowed money for personal indulgence? Never. Not for themselves, not for anyone else—never. Because they know the rule: "What doesn't grow, shrinks." Therefore, they'll never invest borrowed money (especially someone else's) in a passive asset—only in an active one.

The second category of people, when they take out a loan, try to spend it on unattainable or, as they say, status-symbol items. However, they make an obvious logical mistake—things don't create status; they merely reflect it. But can you reflect something that doesn't exist? Investing in expensive phones, cars, or even apartments is investing in a passive asset. The person in this second category isn't investing—they're spending. And they spend precisely on things that, without the loan, would never have crossed their mind to buy. Money burns a hole in their pocket, and they don't really know what they need it for. They fear money and don't like it, justifiably considering it a source of all evil. As you might guess, money responds in kind.

The two categories described above are extremes, b ut they very clearly represent those who possess the right to money and those who do not.

A person from the first category, who possesses the right to money, will multiply it by blending it with their own abilities and talents. They will graft it onto the knowledge of others who possess similar abilities and talents, conducting a unique selection process through such combinations. This is what creates the impression that they make money out of thin air, from seemingly unnoticeable investments. They understand that a harvest can be reaped not only from the field where you planted your seeds, but also from a field that has been pollinated by the fruits grown on your own land—and this is natural to them.

For a person in the second category, this idea is completely unnatural. They cannot comprehend how one can reap a harvest where they did not plant. They firmly believe the opposite: that it is categorically impossible by natural, moral, or ethical laws. Typically, this belief is further reinforced by mental constructs such as, "What God gives, God takes," "We didn't live richly, we won't start now," and, among the more esoterically inclined, they may be convinced that they have become the victim of a resource drainage (kradnik)[1].

However, the accessibility of debt offerings, along with the illusion that "we are all equal," plays a cruel trick on those who do not have the right to money.

---

[1] For more information on resource drainage (kradnik) refer to the chapter on the energy damage in the book by K. Menshikova *"Physical and Energetic Health"*.

The false sense of equality forms the belief in their mind that "we all have the right," and through this belief, they prevent themselves from distinguishing themselves from someone in the first category—the person who truly has that right. The straightforward logic goes: "If Vasya was given a loan and became wealthy, then if I get a loan, I will also become wealthy." They are not concerned with the tools and methods Vasya uses; the person without the right to money lives in a world of simple facts.

The fact that "get-rich-quick" schemes have become widely available is a planned provocation. If people understood this from the outset, they might have been able to protect themselves. But they don't want to understand. And because of this, according to the rules of natural selection, people must go through all the stages of learning, which inevitably leads to the following realization: getting into debt, falling for "quick money" schemes, ending up under the pressure of collectors, and losing what they truly had a right to, is incredibly easy.

Simply put, if you can't calculate how much 2% per day is, you should go back to 3rd grade and catch up on what you missed. But that's just a figure of speech. You can be born with a merchant's sense, or you can finish three specialized financial institutions and still not know anything.

Illusions stem from a lack of understanding of the world you live in and a complete disregard for responsibility towards those you have brought into this world—your children.

If we look at this question of the right to money from the perspective of a caste society[2], the right to money only exists at the level of the merchant caste. It is not expected that the right to money will belong to the laborer caste, since their karmic task is to learn to survive in a constantly changing world and to rid themselves of illusions of stability and the immutability of that very world.

In the merchant caste, a "newcomer" must pass numerous trials and provocations from their own peers, and this task can only be successfully completed if they have already shed all illusions at the previous stage of development and caste formation.

What advice can be given to someone caught in the vice of credit and debt, who recognizes themselves in the description of those who do not have the right to money? Start fresh, including with the debts, and begin to learn to see reality clearly. One must correctly understand their starting position and not live under the illusion that they are truly a warrior by caste, but surrounded by enemies and a total merchant domination. Such an illusion, especially when fueled by bitterness, will only tighten the noose of powerlessness around the neck of the fool.

Those who correctly understood their initial caste positions, by the way, achieved immense financial

---

[2] The caste society will be discussed further in the following pages of this book.

success in a very short time. Why was that? Because understanding the starting point helps to create a practical algorithm for progress—not only to calculate the steps toward achieving the desired outcome but also to prepare adequately for the inevitable provocations that come along the way, and, as a result, to navigate them successfully.

These individuals achieved results quickly, not only entering the merchant caste but also securing their place within it with full rights. The rapid success was, of course, also due to the fact that at the merchant level, the vector of progress did not stop; it carried them further. Merchant status is a necessary step in the natural development of society for those who see and understand the entire hierarchical ladder.

On the other hand, those who built their vector based on the illusion that they were something they were not, received nothing—and that was in the best-case scenario. In the worst-case scenario, their lives would enter a severe crisis from which they would not recover their reality for a long time.

At every caste level, a person does not simply prove something in a game or battle. At each level, they acquire the necessary qualities without which survival at the next level would be impossible. How can a laborer enter the merchant caste if they do not understand the laws of the world's structure and manifestation? If they do not see or feel the dynamic of change? If they truly fear people to the point of cramping and convulsions, and this fear makes them passively compliant with everything? How can one make money if they do not understand people and are afraid of them? How can one make money in a world where the concept of "money" exists only in the realm of people?

The conclusion is simple: correctly determine your position. If every day you understand your current starting point, you will have everything you need—and fairly quickly.

This rule is especially relevant for those attempting to fast-track their path of growth, using "magical catalysts"—practices, rituals, mechanisms for developing consciousness and magical abilities. The correct understanding of your place within the social system in magic is a starting test—a test of honesty. For in magic, lies are not permissible.

Fatamorgana: I was raised, like all Soviet children, on the ideals of selfless labor. My relatives used to say that I was lazy and would never achieve anything in life, except inherit my grandmother's house in the village. I once got angry at such a remark and took offense. It was probably then that I decided for myself that I wouldn't live the way they did. In the end, I succeeded.

The work on the topic of money stirred sharp pain and a burning sensation between my shoulder blades, bringing me to tears. The next day, my sacrum and lower back hurt. And my throat. I kept wanting to drink—tea, water, even beer, although I don't like it. In any case, I'll have to revisit this topic on the next levels of study. For now, the main blockage looks like this: "What? Work again? How much more do I have to do? I don't know where or how to start. And how can I, just a simple village girl, reach the highest level of prosperity?" Then, I saw a report in the subway about Russian women on the Forbes list. They are just like me—village girls, factory workers, from the outskirts of cities. And somehow, they made it. It helped. And it seemed like a good omen.

I started clearing out fears and blockages related to laziness. Again, the burning between my shoulder blades. I breathed through it and gathered all the sensations. I will continue to clear these beliefs and unprocessed emotions.

Another interesting observation: the idea is now quite popular—"Why did we study? We never worked in our field anyway." Or even, "Why waste time on education when you can start earning right away?" I realized that school, university, and graduate school were probably the most valuable experiences and investments of time. I don't remember the details of what and how I studied, but during my work now, I noticed that time seems to have become monolithic. I draw skills from there, like working with information, finding and reading the right books, and analyzing. To honestly go through and work through the first lessons of GTM[3] is no task for the faint of heart. But I remembered my student years, sat down, read, drew diagrams, and came up with options. I also learned to express my thoughts clearly and coherently. In the end, education helped me escape from abject poverty. It greatly increased my life potential. Strength of materials and the theory of electromagnetic fields, in and of themselves, are very enriching. And I was also afraid of failing my studies, not passing exams, so, out of fear, I graduated with honors. In my first year, I lost about 15 kilograms. I clung to that opportunity with everything I had, just to avoid returning to where I had come from.

But now I know how rights are earned in this world. And that, too, is an invaluable skill and knowledge I gained over the years of my education.

For a long time, I seriously wanted to buy a motorcycle and take long trips—far and for a long time. I worked through this desire, as well as the financial aspect of the matter, using my methods.

My friends advised me to watch videos from a popular motorblogger. So, I watched. At first, it seemed like a waste of time—I already knew everything about the rules, laws, and speed limits. Otherwise, sooner or later, a concrete guardrail would embrace you. Eventually, I understood what I really wanted. Clearly, it

---

[3] The course "General Theory of Magic" is available for free on Menshikova's YouTube channel and on the "MAGIC UNITED" forum.

wasn't to just ride to the store or the nearby village market. It wasn't even about a trip to Mongolia.

I also realized that everything in life has a price. And my motorcycle dream—too. My personal trigger was revealed: I'm not ready to do some things that need to be done on the road, or to be morally prepared to do them. And this means that I wouldn't be able to react appropriately in a certain situation and would create a dangerous situation—perhaps even end up in the guardrail. So, for now, I'll stick to walking.

These videos, along with the AB[4] cleanings, saved me a lot of time, money, nerves, and perhaps even my life.

Gregory: Money... They really say that the work on this topic is not about monetary signs, but about the right—your true right, not one invented by you. And this is where those fears arise because you want so much, but when you think about it—what will you do with it? How much more will it cost you, and how many problems will follow? As people say, "We didn't live richly, so we won't start now." To avoid these fears, one must clearly understand their own point of reference, with all the consequences that follow. I searched for mine for a long time, and then I realized: why am I looking so low, not

---

[4] AB — Astral Body. The method of cleaning the Astral Body is an effective way to rid the consciousness of unconstructive fears and long-held resentments. It is taught in the 2nd course of the Main Department of the School.

lifting my head? I've created all these fears for myself. That's when things started to shift...

Ilya 444: Ksenia Menshikova is one of the very few who has a clear, well-thought-out methodology for teaching. I think at this stage, we don't fully understand the entire structure of the education. There are still things that aren't entirely clear to me either. After some reflection, I accepted her thesis—not to reject any experience... Money and social achievements will likely serve as a criterion for assessing successful learning (alongside other factors).

Owl: I disagree with you. It seems to me that money shouldn't be included in the criteria for evaluation at all. How can money be a measure for someone just starting their magical path?

Ilya 444: Money (prosperity) is directly related to magical development. How can one master higher currents if they can't even control the lower ones[5]? I believe the current of money is something a beginner practitioner should master first. If they succeed, that's the result; if not, there's no magic. And most importantly, if the issue of prosperity isn't solved, if there's poverty, then how can any development take place? All energy

---

[5] For more details on the currents of forces, refer to the book by K. Menshikova, *"Egregores and the System of Controlling Reality"*.

and time will be spent on searching for the resources for survival. A needy mage raises questions…

Stinger: What conclusions should a descendant of a wealthy and prosperous family draw (whose family has never lacked and has helped others) if they personally have money problems? Specifically, the collapse of a business… Where would you suggest starting?

Hannibal: You always have to start with yourself. If there's order with money in the entire family, but only you don't have it, then you must first try to analyze where these rights were lost. Maybe in some situation, the person willingly or wrongly mismanaged them, and that's why they were taken away. After that, clean yourself and restore them.

QuizzyBuzz: Good day, colleagues. As a good addition to the topic of money and working with it, I would like to recommend the following documentary: "Capital in the Twenty-First Century." A brief historical overview. Present and future. An overview that will allow you to truly feel the topic. This is definitely recommended.

Tatiana, a student: My great-grandfather was a Transbaikal Cossack, a hero of World War I, a fairly prosperous man, but he didn't want to give his property to the collective farm. In 1930, he joined what was known as the "kulak uprising," for which he was killed by Soviet authorities. This means that the property, which was forcibly taken from him, should be returned to my family by the system. And with interest! My husband's family, ethnic Germans from the Volga region, owned steamboats. As you can imagine, they were later expropriated by the Soviet government, and the large family was exiled to the Kazakh steppes to live in dugouts they dug themselves. It was the ground squirrels that saved them from dying of hunger. Another debt to the system. By the way, the German government, when accepting ethnic Germans for permanent residence, pays them a substantial compensation in euros for the hardships they had to endure in Russia.

Natalia: Following the reasoning, one might suggest a logical connection: "A implies B" = "The system forcibly took from my ancestors, therefore, the system owes me." According to the classic laws of mathematical logic, by the rule of contraposition, we have: "Not B implies not A" = "If the system doesn't repay the debt, it means the ancestors willingly gave up their rights." So, if you claim that "the system must return what it took from my family, and with interest," it's hardly surprising that the bank should have not only withheld interest but also suggested not returning the principal at all. As an alternative, very few could endure such hardships, and it's quite possible that the ancestors voluntarily gave up their rights. And it could be as simple as a tiny phrase: "Take everything—just let me live." Perhaps the family history needs to be examined more closely. I invite discussion. I don't claim to have the truth.

Yllymakh: You've raised an interesting topic! I have a similar story: my ancestors were very wealthy landowners from Bashkiria, and they were also dispossessed in 1930. There was absolutely no talk of voluntarily giving up their rights. My great-grandmother was shot in front of small children, including my six-year-old grandmother, right in the yard. The entire family, labeled as relatives of an active resistor, was exiled to Uzbekistan with the full confiscation of property for ten years, and after their exile, they were banned from settling in Bashkiria. Almost all of the children died in exile.

Being a historian by education and spirit, I decided to dig into this branch of my family—but it wasn't easy. Apparently, to cover their tracks, people burned all the archives. I can't even find any official documentation proving my grandmother's birth. However, I easily uncovered information about another branch of the family—the Cossack side, which lived just two hundred kilometers away from these relatives. They never had any problems with the government—no one was de-Cossackized, no one was exiled, and throughout the war, they lived with their own cow. No state official ever thought to take that cow. They also went to church without persecution. And even though they lived literally next door to the other—much more suffering—branch of the family, it was as though they existed in two parallel realities.

Returning to the present day, a question arose: could these difficult relations within the family determine the complicated relationships with the state? Clearly, the family has a right to money, but for some reason, not everyone can access it. Half of my relatives live peacefully under any regime and even manage to integrate successfully into its institutions. My branch, on the other hand, is in constant persecution. Everything the state touches goes to ruin! It's not even about financial and property losses—though they have been enormous—but about the physical persecution by the state—false accusations and imprisonments (thankfully, they were released before trial, after a few years in detention), and when robbed or killed, it's actually terrifying to go to the police because they will just lock you up... I'm seriously wondering if my distant ancestors were involved in organizing some kind of coup, invasion, or uprising against the Russian state in ancient times? It really seems like it hates us. What's interesting is that the branch suffering the most from the state's actions is the one that most resembles my great-grandmother, who was shot in 1930. Other relatives cooperate with the system without any problems.

Tatiana, a student: Yllymakh, what else did you do besides contacting the archives? Did you manage to connect with your great-grandmother (the one who was shot) and her family?

Yllymakh: The entire maternal line is very responsive but highly emotional. There's a good connection during meditation, but it's mostly tears and snot... I can't make out words yet. I found an interesting sigil for a candle invocation—haven't tried it yet, but I plan to. The contact with my grandmother is normal—I can hear her and feel her presence during the invocation. I haven't asked her about the ancestors yet, though. I have a ton of questions about them.

Guest: Could the surrounding environment affect one's prosperity?

Alexey Kobelev: It can influence a lot, indeed! It has long been observed that a person's income is equal to the average income of the ten people around them. Try introducing someone with money into your social circle—and your income will increase. Similarly, if you remove people who have money problems from your circle, the likelihood of a positive result increases. Moreover, money is one of the lower streams of energy. If someone's financial issue isn't resolved, then likely all other higher streams will also be disrupted. So, cleaning up your environment isn't just important—it's crucial.

The thing is, people will begin to drift away from you if you move forward. First, they'll laugh at you, then there will be aggression, and eventually, they'll all disappear. But in their place will come new people who resonate with you, bringing both wealth and growth. But ultimately, it all depends on you.

Guest: Thank you! Subconsciously, I feel that my environment is holding me back. In fact, quite strongly. There's another question. I've noticed that whenever I come up with a project or even just an idea to go somewhere and I tell one of my friends about it, it always falls through. Later, I heard from a business coach: "If I want something not to work out, I tell people about it." I don't understand how this works.

Vasilisa: When you think about a project, you saturate it with your energy, you create a space for this idea, and you work through some details—how to do it, what to do. Gradually, the idea takes on a more tangible form. During communication, people exchange energy and project images. When you tell someone about your ideas, you are voluntarily opening up your space, inviting your listeners in, and giving away your energy through your storytelling. Perhaps you are naturally a donor, and you've found a group of "eaters." This is something only you can judge. This situation teaches discipline, teaching you not to talk about your plans. Another analogy: an idea requires nurturing and maturation before manifestation, like pregnancy. If you interfere with the process of pregnancy, it risks a miscarriage.

Axel: Good afternoon, friends! In the seminar on the topic of money, Ksenia Evgenievna talks about the need to develop control over your time through planning. The further ahead we plan, the better we control our time, and thus, we increase our level of prosperity. But what should we do when, in response to planning, we face opposition from external circumstances, not just internal ones? For example, I have no fear of planning a year ahead, or even two. But even when I plan for the next day, events occur that prevent the plan from happening. And it happens in a rather harsh form. For instance, I make plans to meet someone next week, and the day before our meeting, they get hit by a car and end up in the hospital for two months. Then we make another plan, and their office burns down, etc. The company signs a contract to service a building—and the building burns down a week later. If the goals don't involve other people or objects, then when it's time to start the task, either circumstances won't allow it, or, if you over-prepare, your body simply shuts down, feeling powerless and drowsy. You just fall and can't get up for half a day. What might be the cause of such a situation?

Zebreva Natalia: First of all, because your plans directly depend on specific people. We live among people and interact with them, and in our projects, there are always people involved. But when you rely on one person, the entire project depends on that one individual. These significant obstacles may be connected to your attempt to move to a higher level, and you are not familiar with the new rules of the game. So, you give up, staying at your current level.

VladimirA: It all started for me a long time ago, without seminars, just by writing down even seemingly trivial plans (to the point of absurdity, like "open eyes")—wake up—mark it consciously and with a checkmark in the organizer as "done," brush teeth—done, go to work—done... and so on. For a start, it's not too difficult, but making it regular so that your planner pages are filled with checkmarks and notes of "done." Once it becomes possible to accomplish at least ten points on your list, you can start adding more complex tasks to your plans: "meeting with Vasya," "finally wash the windows," "sign a contract for 1 million," "change the world," "plant a tree"—the key is to create the reality that what's written in the plans is actually done and confirmed with checkmarks.

Oksash: Colleagues, I'll share my approach to working through the issue of planning and implementing what's planned. I wrote a work plan for today and started following it, but if obstacles arise, I don't force the situation, I make another attempt. If another obstacle comes up, I interpret it as higher forces—or something else—being against me doing this *today*. I move it to the next day. I don't force circumstances—it's energy-draining and undermines my strength and self-confidence. But I don't give up on my plans either—I wait for the right wind.

For example: you plan to wash the windows today, but the hot water gets turned off... Two possible scenarios: you wash with cold water (which could make you sick), or you heat the water (which takes more time). What to do? Wash or not wash? A strong-willed person might say: "I've decided—I'll do it!" and start following the plan strictly. They wash the windows, feel pleased for overcoming the "difficulties," and then find out that they've turned the hot water back on! It was off for just a couple of hours. Maybe it would have been better to wait and tackle something else from your plan for the day? Maybe you're being tested for flexibility and patience? Or maybe there's something more important at the moment that you don't see?

Toria: I understand now that the higher a person rises, the less chaos surrounds them. They learn to control and calm this chaos, holding it in check with their consciousness. Regarding planning: the first time I felt heaviness after working through the connection between money and planning, I felt resistance, rejection, even though I do enjoy writing and fixing things for myself. There is still a difference between planning and recording events. Now, I've calmly accepted it and will work on not only recording but also planning. I'll see how long I can maintain this. I liked a colleague's example of writing everything down in a notebook. At the same time, I read elsewhere about a practice of constantly writing down ALL your plans and desires. I want to try it.

Before studying at the School, my principle was: "Destiny knows what I need," and I just flowed with life, ultimately getting no results. Thanks to the education at the School, I'm changing myself and my life.

Fatamorgana: I also started breaking things down this way: we don't have money. But the truth is, we did have money. In books, for a rainy day, for the future. My mother planned to move with me to another city after my school, once I got into university. We didn't really have money in 1993, and again in 1998. At that point, I had to leave for another city alone, live independently, and earn money to get an education. It was painful back then, wondering why things were the way they were. But now I understand how much of a blessing it was: breaking free from my mother's care, struggling on my own since I was 16, gaining experience. Perhaps that life circumstance helped shape my new attitude toward money. There was always just enough. It always came from somewhere. I stopped saving just to save. If I did save, it was for something specific. And I spent or invested. I completely abandoned credit cards— I closed them all.

Blagoyar: Looking back, I truly realized that all my financial success came hand in hand with planning, analytics, and forecasting. This was true both in developing my own business and in my employment—where I focused on perfecting my craft and found many skills that could be learned even in seemingly menial physical jobs.

When I first became a manager in a painting workshop, I was initially uncomfortable, since I had worked for myself for a long time before that. But then I became absorbed in fine-tuning the process, which was in a pitiful state. After working on it, outlining, and launching this production, I quickly lost interest in the already well-established system. At the same time, I was led, somewhat reluctantly, into the world of magic... and from being a very valuable colleague, I quickly became the most inconvenient one.

I'm interested in the question: if I am an antagonist to the system, and material wealth is largely provided by egregorial structures, what should I do? Meanwhile, I am involved in restoring pagan traditions, essentially being an enemy of the current system. How can I address the material aspect of things?

VarvaraNjord: Hello, Blagoyar. Have you read the book *"Egregores"*[6] by Ksenia Evgenievna? It discusses

---

[6] Reference to the book by K. Menshikova *"Egregores and the System of Controlling Reality"*.

the levels of egregores. Specifically, there is the level of the state and ministries, and there is the level of spontaneous and professional egregores. When it comes to money, it's important to understand your own god and their particularities. There are open videos about this. For example, if you are Phoebus[7] and your god is Odin, then you receive money directly from the government, from the source. But if you are Hecate, then it would be off the official record. Money, like health, is a current that comes when your system works correctly and is aligned with the active core.

If you are the antagonist of that system, you need to understand your own system—what nourishes it, what goals it has—and find the space and work where your system can achieve those goals. You've already described this experience, focusing on your success and skill development in your past jobs. That's what you need to latch onto and develop further. Why did you need those skills? What values were behind them? Based on what you've shared, it seems like you might be Dionysus—who are indeed the antagonists in any system. They are the ones who seek and develop algorithms for freedom and avoidance of the influence of Phoebus's systems. There are many open videos from Menshikova about these two channels, including those on money.

---

[7] For more information about those born on the channels of Phoebus or Dionysus, see addendum 1 at the end of this book.

To answer your question directly, you absolutely need to find the egregorial structure that aligns most closely with your goals and, through an agreement with it, receive the necessary resources to achieve those goals. There are many different spontaneous and professional egregores, and one of them will surely be a good fit for you. A profession itself is also an egregore—perhaps this is the one you need to interact with (and the skill development might have been precisely for this purpose), not with the spontaneous (organization).

Self-knowledge and strengthening your system is such an interesting and productive endeavor! You're just in a transition phase—from the old, where you were suited to others, to the new, where there's still much to develop. But these developments will come. The people and work in your new self-awareness will certainly appear.

Ekaterina NM: Probably, Blagoyar, you are one of those people who enter the system to create something new or restore the old, but not the dysfunctional. At the same time, you are studying the entire process of what you're doing. While the activity is new and developing you, it's interesting to you, and you genuinely want to participate in the process of becoming. As soon as what you're doing becomes self-sustaining, you lose interest and the drive for what you were previously involved in. The pattern imposed by society says that this is the wrong approach. It seems that you shouldn't do anything anymore, just sit back and shovel money in. But no, that doesn't satisfy you, and that's when a dissonance may arise in your mind.

If you understand and recognize this characteristic in yourself, you will leave your comfortable place for another. If not, you will subconsciously create the conditions for the space itself to push you out. This reflects your need for growth and new experiences. This approach to work develops you and increases your beingness. If you allow yourself to constantly gain new experiences, without clinging to the old, it will help you grow. As you develop, you increase your EV[8] (Existential Volume). The higher your EV, the more valuable your time becomes.

I didn't see in your description that you are an antagonist to the system. You come in and change something, studying the process. But you can't remain in a stable, static place that doesn't require change. You are in places that demand change and are new to you. The condition is quite simple: if you gain new knowledge, new experiences—then you thrive; if you don't, then you don't.

Learn to catch the moment when the egregorial system stops developing you and providing you with something new. This is the moment when it's time to move on to another place, or if you're still attached to

---

[8] EV — Existential Volume. This term defines the quantitative characteristic of useful experience, which, in turn, serves as the basis for determining social status and/or caste affiliation.

the old, create something new and interesting within it. When you feel emotions of boredom or the "same-old-day" sensation, that's a clear sign that it's time to move on.

Pagan gods can bring resources to a person—that does not hinder material well-being. Polytheistic systems are the enemy of monotheistic systems, but not of all egregores in general.

Menshikova: You should not equate the concepts of "money" and "wealth." As long as you think this way, you won't understand the concepts themselves, nor the egregorial foundation behind these phenomena. Let's start with terminology, as usual.

An egregore is a governing idea. At its core, there is an idea—maximally all-encompassing.

Now let's try to understand: what is the idea of wealth or money? A brief reflection will inevitably lead to the understanding that the idea of wealth better aligns with egregorial requirements—it is abstract, prolonged over time, and never fully attainable (meaning, again, in time).

In contrast, the idea of money is fleeting, specific, and—most importantly—measurable, whereas wealth is very difficult to measure, since any measure will not be universal and will depend on philosophy and religious worldview.

From this, the conclusion follows: the egregore of wealth exists, while the egregore of money is an illusion, a phantom egregore, a mirage in the desert for those who are tired and have failed to find the idea of their life. Money is just a tool and a lure for those who make it the meaning of their existence.

It's quite simple: if in egregore A, element X is a tool, and in egregore B, element X is an idea, the meaning of life (the core), then egregore A is ontologically stronger than egregore B and has the right to use it without asking for permission, as its own tool. Or, to express it mathematically, egregore A is the set, and egregore B is an element of that set—one among many.

Wealth, as an idea, is possession. It implies the use of many measures and tools. But this idea is not a fetish in itself; it is merely a reflection of more global ideas.

My advice, dear colleagues and students: never make an idea that is finite and/or measurable the core of your existence. This is the key not only to ensuring you never become a tool of any egregorial system but also to approaching the understanding of your god's power. In the goal-setting of any mind that has entered the game on the territory of Mother Earth, the goal is precisely possession. The question is: possession of what?

Returning to the idea of money. The concept of "money current," which we use when working with currents, is an occult-magical term that should never be taken literally. It's more like prosperity, but even this term is imperfect, as prosperity implies a certain static nature (a fixed property that can be measured). But a current is a current. A process. So, when we speak of the current of money, we are speaking of the process of creating space with specific unchanging properties while still possessing the quality of movement and fluidity.

The current of money is a space for the materialization of other currents and the fixation of the results of possession.

No matter how spiritual and advanced a person may be, the fact that they live in an entirely social world must be taken into account. And to survive, a person needs money. Those who develop themselves in magic must be able to provide for their needs without being distracted from their main work. Money, in this world, is a measure of social success and, at times, a measure of talent and ability, even potential. Therefore, a mage must learn to attract this current of money in order not to waste their life and time on the basic task of acquiring resources.

What is money from the perspective of the current of energy? Money is materialized energy. Their materiality only comes from the agreement that people once made with each other, agreeing on a price. As energy currents pass through a socially structured space, they materialize as money. Thus, money is the equivalent of the value of force in the world of humans.

Attracting the current of energy in the form of money is not particularly difficult. The more difficult task is to lock it in on yourself, direct it to your system, to your goals. Very few people are naturally endowed with this quality. The rest must learn.

For example, a current of money passes through a person, through their consciousness and field, and in a relatively large volume. But this person has no tools to hold this current, to transform it through their goals and tasks, and send it further. People like this are said to have money "slip through their fingers."

Why does this happen?

It happens to people who have no personal goal, no clearly defined personal value. All the goals they set for themselves are not their own. For the current of money, they become a kind of pipe, with a third party standing at the exit, having the goal. The conduit person attracted the current of money due to their inherent abilities, but someone else made use of it. The conduit person often doesn't even notice the massive current of energy passing through them, as they don't see it. Just like a pipe, which doesn't know whether it's carrying oil, water, or sewage.

From the book by K. Menshikova
"Egregores and the System of Controlling Reality".

THE CURRENT OF MONEY

To understand the nature of this current, it is necessary to return to the topic of changing perception and altering terminology. In a magical sense, the current of money is not the quantity of paper or other manifested material goods, but rather an informational potential that possesses the ability to materialize ideas. In other words, it is the ability to create something out of nothing. It is the ability to instantly draw the necessary energetic resource to oneself and materialize it into a specific, manifested form.

This potential can be expressed in the amount of banknotes or other numbers, or it may not; it can take the familiar form visible to the human eye, or it can be entirely invisible to societal assessment. The current of money is the potential to direct life force toward altering the form of manifested reality.

Materialization is always a one-way process, and it has no reverse force. Just as you cannot push a born child back into the womb, so too can that which has been manifested in the material world not be turned back into potential energy—it begins to possess its own energy. This is a current that moves outward into the world in one direction. Therefore, the potential to attract life forces, which is the essence of the current of money, lies in the fact that this renewable process exists not due to the return of the environment after an investment in materialization, but due to the constant activity of internal sources—movement of informational currents within the system, their manifested conflict.

The return of the environment is an effect, not the cause of the appearance of the current of money. It is an indicator, but not the foundation for the current's continuation. Just as a reflection in a mirror shows that you are not a vampire, but a fully living being, it does not guarantee that this will always be the case.

In manifested reality, the current of money is the potential to take a resource, applied to the resource itself. Here, the limitations may be more distorted than in the limitation of the current of health: when consciousness is limited in the right to the current of health, egregores can only affect one element—the individual's consciousness—blocking its potential. However, no egregorial system has the right, nor the ability, to affect life force or the power of the earth.

When it comes to limiting the current of money, as the right and potential to materialize ideas, the system uses a two-level method: it affects both the resource and the potential, as both are already the property of the system and are not directly related to the currents of the earth's force.

The influence on the resource comes from the egregorial level of the government. It not only determines the form and value of the resource but also regulates the limits of distribution across all lower levels of the egregorial hierarchy. By emphasizing the primacy of form, this influence reduces the significance of the essence of the current itself, making it practically invisible and unknowable. Sometimes, the form becomes so elaborate and phenomenally powerful that it separates itself from the essence, allowing the essence to exist independently from the form.

The form of the money current is opaque and often does not allow one to see that the vessel can be filled with anything. If the vessel is labeled "water," no one will check the truth of the label, because people are conditioned to use the form, not the essence. For example, if a banknote says 100 rubles, very few people will check the authenticity of what is written: whether the paper holds any real backing (security) beyond the official information and the "honest word" of the issuing bank.

Influence on the potential is a restriction or allowance for the manifestation of the right to materialize, either in accordance with the permitted form or in any other.

Thus, the money current turns out to be an artificial current, present in our world as a product of an agreement, with the chosen form being merely a conve-

Egregorial Hierarchy

nient representation of it for people. Without a specific contractual form, the current of money could be called the current of prosperity. However, the presence of form specifies prosperity, describing in the world of humans what can be considered and named prosperity, and what cannot.

The form in which the current manifests is determined by the egregorial system, specifically by the level of the government. The consent of the bearer of the potential—the person—toward this form automatically signifies their agreement to the limits set by the system, namely: agreeing that the "lord of the form" has the right to influence both the resource and the potential. It is the rigid attachment to the form that not only prevents one from increasing the limits of allowed materialization but even from fully utilizing the already existing ones.

A person is the continuation of their god's mind, meaning they are the bearer of the currents of forces, operating at the level where their divine essence functions (or functioned). However, by entering into a contract with religion (through baptism or initiation) and with the state (by accepting its laws and agreeing with them), a person inevitably grants these structures the right to influence the natural currents of forces. In the case of the government, this is merely consent to the limits and form, but at the level of religions, it is a complete transfer of rights over the basic currents of forces, and, consequently, an inability to use it freely (the slave has no rights to property or freedom). From this point on, a person cannot manifest the potential of the current of prosperity (money) beyond the limits, norms, and rules set by those who define the form.

Thus, the acquisition of the money current depends on two factors:
1. How deeply the consciousness is embedded within the system of religion and the government.
2. At which hierarchical level within the egregorial environment the person's consciousness operates.

When the first factor is present, the second becomes highly relevant, because the first presupposes the person's agreement to accept the current of money only in the specific form defined by the "patron" and according to established rules. Formally, a person agrees that the government, and only the government, is the source of the money current if they firmly tie this current to the manifested form. In this case, the second rule predetermines that proximity to the source will yield a greater current, and distance will result in a smaller one. Thus, a person operating at the egregorial level of the government or financial and social institutions will have access to a larger volume of the current than someone whose consciousness operates at the level of their family or spontaneous egregores, because the distribution of this formalized current goes from top to bottom, splitting into finer currents at each lower level.

If the egregorial level of the government had the ability to influence not just the resource but also the potential, the distribution would occur differently than it does now—more evenly, both spatially and temporally—since the government values stability and the preservation of what has been achieved more than the ideological struggle and the risks associated with it. But since people themselves willingly give up their rights to the egregorial level of religions, the government must take this into account—it will have to coordinate its actions with the religious level and, to a greater or lesser extent, allow the influence of religious teachings and dogmas on the formation of laws.

Since the right to a resource in this world holds more value and weight than mere immediate possession of it, the hierarchical position of religions becomes even more established over the government level. Religions do not directly regulate the rules for resource distribution or, in most cases, interfere with legislation on this matter, but they set the fundamental principle: equally or unequally, evenly or unevenly. Modern religions say: not equally, not evenly: the favored ones (the righteous) should receive more, while the others less. All Abrahamic religions, having originated from the same source, introduce the principle of inequality into the state systems where they have succeeded in parasitizing or openly leading. On one hand, this is not necessarily bad—the principle itself may be necessary for the current level of human development. However, the rules through which this principle manifests completely distort its true meaning, just as the form of money distorts its essence.

The right that people voluntarily give to the religious system is the right to their god's current, the right to manifest it on the earthly level, the right to "fertilize" it with this current to birth something new and necessary. If a person is included in the religious egregore and has the right to manifest their godly current, they can only do so with the permission of their religious matrix and according to its rules.

The experiment conducted in the Soviet Union—to abolish religion and reduce it to a taxable structure—showed the effects of such abolition, specifically in terms of the money current: everyone received gradually, but equally. Rights were determined not by holiness, but by loyalty, not by servility, but by deeds. However, in such a commune, there was also the flip side of the coin—the lack of space for competitive struggle and, as a result, the failure to apply the principle of natural selection.

When the principle of natural selection is not allowed to fully influence the processes of evolution, the object (in this case, people) is as if in "sterile" conditions, not receiving viruses, provocations, or injections from outside. Its immune system does not develop, and consciousness mutates in the closed space of sterility. After some time, such mutation makes the slightest informational virus capable of destroying it. This is exactly what happened in the USSR: the completely closed Iron Curtain blocked all disturbing information, achieving a kind of sterility, but a breach was found, which led to the justified collapse—diseased minds of millions of people in the severe form of informational poisoning.

Sterile conditions are needed only in a laboratory where experiments are conducted. For life, in its natural development, it is necessary to receive contacts with everything else, which the currents of necessary chaos bring for development.

Chaos manifests itself in the informational system of the egregorial world and the formation of energy currents, not so much by its unpredictability, but through the appearance of new qualities in this world, which directly relate to the money current. Since this current, as it turns out, is nothing other than an agreement, let's clarify the true nature of this agreement.

If you make another effort to step away from the form of the money current, you will more easily recognize its original essence: the materialization of higher informational currents coming from the gods; the potential turned into a result. This is the need for the manifestation of the higher, "elder" currents—on one hand. And on the other hand, it is the need of Mother Earth, the principle of natural selection, as a property of life, a universal method of the ecosystem's work in constant development striving for immortality.

The combination of these two principles gives us a clarification of the agreement, as the game of aspirations: the money current, at its core, is the manifestation of properties. Properties of the consciousnesses of people, each of whom has their own god and their own currents of forces.

Chaos is dangerous for static reality not only because of its unpredictability, but also because its presence always introduces new properties into this world, causing the value of the old to inevitably diminish. In order to withstand competition, as a trial of novelty, already manifested properties must endlessly develop, and any development is only possible when there is comparison.

Snorrik: This information is astonishing, very useful! I immediately understood many of my problems. The right to money, debts, castes, etc. I used to subconsciously feel that money is a resource not available to everyone and not in full. What K. Menshikova was saying, I had guessed or heard in other informational resources, but her information is truly a revelation! I would like to break the vicious cycle of debt, and I will work on this. My ancestors were right in forbidding borrowing money! Especially if you "enter" the wrong caste, as I understand it, punishment or testing often happens through the financial sphere. Unfortunately, in our occult "world," there are many different practices for working with money, financial currents, varying in quality and often of low caliber. At the same time, they seem to focus on "treating symptoms, not the disease itself."

Admin: "However, it would be a mistake to perceive a 'failed' nature and such an incarnation as a misfortune or, worse, as a punishment. It is not imprisonment, nor shackles. It is additional conditions for development, necessary systemic difficulties. It is a specific space in which the soul's structure must learn to assert its right to shape goals as it needs. If you include the regime of greatest favor, no learning will take place:

any useful skill becomes a right only when a person has proven three times that they will not betray it, will not break under the weight of problems. Therefore, it is correct to view unfavorable life conditions simply as a necessary testing environment.

If you learn to see life this way, not only will human success but also magical development of consciousness become accessible to you. The higher the soul's task, the more obstacles it must overcome and the greater the pressure of events it must withstand without breaking.

Thus, the reality we now begin to consider from a slightly different perspective should be viewed as nothing but a testing program, in which everyone must undergo trials according to their personal task." From *"Goals and Values"* by Menshikova.

Natalia: The master of their rights, having realized that they were once manipulated, can demand them back by right of ownership, but how does that work if they were misled?

Vasilisa: It's unlikely that such demands will be satisfied, but who says you can't try? Manipulating and provoking is not prohibited. Those with rights need to prove that they are resistant to provocations and not swayed by anyone's tricks. Menshikova has a video on kradniks—she goes into great detail about it. In turn, if you know who took your rights, you can try to make them return them—provoke them to give it back.

Anastasiya: Hello, forum members. I wanted to ask, how should one deal with debtors who refuse to repay their debts?

Yllymakh: Debt is a channel of communication with the debtor, no doubt. But don't view the question emotionally—"They hurt me, I want revenge!" So, some questions:
- What caused the debt? Was it your mistake in distributing the resource? Is it your debt from a past life? Is it a non-material debt for which you could be asked for material compensation? Was there an error in maintaining the protection of your system? What was the true cause of the debt? What preconditions led to this situation? Ultimately, who is more to blame—you or the debtor—for the circumstances that have developed?
- What will you gain by taking revenge? Will your BM increase, decrease, will you achieve justice, or will you disturb the balance? What are the consequences of carrying out your plan, and what if you don't? Will you lose rights or preserve them?

If specific methods of influence are needed, there are plenty on the BMAR[9] website. I think there are enough ideas for two dozen debtors.

Guest: Dear teachers and fellow students, please help me understand. It seems that I am now in the process of restoring my rights to money. Against the background of a stable and steady average financial position, after starting my studies at the School, very attractive job offers began to appear. I accepted all of them, but after three months, one of the three jobs has become a thorn in my side. I just don't feel right about it, even though it pays better than the others. If I quit, I won't regret it. I have no attachment to the money. But won't this look like a voluntary renunciation of my rights to money? Or am I looking at this from the wrong angle, and instead of restoring my rights, is this an attempt by external forces to shift my focus toward financial interests at the expense of development? I spend no more than 2-3 hours a day on all my jobs, and my focus remains on studying. Please help me sort this out.

Hannibal: I'm reminded of our Don Juan: "Does this path have a heart? If it does, it's a good path; if it doesn't, it's of no use." But the most important thing is not to make a mistake. If I were in your place, I would

---

[9] Forum for both beginners and practitioners, "Black Magic and Runes."

investigate the reason why you don't like it. Is it contradicting your values and your I Am[10], or perhaps it's an energy-draining task, and your astral body doesn't want to release energy? In other words—laziness, which then causes a complex of unpleasant sensations. Renouncing money for the sake of your I Am is sacred, and no current will leave you because of this; on the contrary, your significance in this world will increase. But if you're renouncing because of your weaknesses, it may offend and leave, saying "you couldn't handle it."

Guest: When this offer came, I was interested in the new experience. I saw it as a sign. There is practically no labor or energy expenditure, but over time, I saw complete confusion and instability in the project's leadership. The goal is simply to get rich quickly, with no concern for what will happen afterward. I'm not fond of that attitude. I prefer slow, gradual development and achieving clearly defined goals. Here, there's too much pointless fuss and chaos. I value order. And what bothers me most is the disorderliness of the leadership. Now, I feel like even for these 1–2 hours a day, there's some kind of parasite sucking my energy. I feel like I'll leave, and everything will fall apart. I think it's time. Thanks to everyone for their responses.

Kharakternik: Several questions:

---

[10] I Am — a state of self-awareness, a touch with one's true essence.

1. For example, a person had a position, some status, but then they are dismissed, go to the unemployment office, and receive benefits—could this be considered a voluntary renunciation of rights to money?

2. Moving on, a person is offered a position but refuses it in favor of someone else—does this count as giving up their rights?

3. Let's talk about magic. A person practices, gains experience, but then, due to some events or their own foolishness, decides to abandon it for many years—does this count as giving up their magical rights?

4. How can one understand the boundary, the point at which they are giving up their rights versus simply showing weakness without losing their rights?

Yllymakh: Let's go step by step.

1. I think there's some truth to this. Who goes to the unemployment office? Mostly manual workers and graduates. The logic is clear—one group needs a little extra cash, the other is unsure of their abilities. But! Have you seen many confident people standing in line at the unemployment office? Or former officials? Or top specialists? Probably not. Even students hustle around, trying to realize themselves. The unemployment office is about shifting responsibility for your employment, your future, and your life onto the state. When you shift responsibility, you always give up your rights. To solve your problem with your own rights, the state will resolve

it. Once they solve it, your right will remain with whoever solved your problem. At least, that's how I see it.

2. Yes, if you have no alternative. If there is an alternative, it's simply a refusal.

3. With magic, it doesn't work like that. Your weakness—your refusal—will be used by magic against you. That is, you will be drawn into such a series of events where you will have no choice—only magic will save you. However, if even under mounting pressure, you refuse to use/change to magic three times during planned provocations, then it's all over. Ksenia Evgenievna commented on a similar issue in one of her videos.

4. As I understand it, and colleagues can correct me if I'm wrong, the test is carried out three times during planned provocations. You are given the right to make mistakes and time to correct them. After the first provocation, there is a second one, and then a third. If you refuse the struggle three times and succumb to temptation, then it's your problem. Your right is taken. And they gain rights in the same way—not less than three tests for the right to possess the right. The algorithm solidifies after three repetitions.

Kharakternik: I am trying to understand what constitutes provocation. For example, a situation: a person quits a familiar job, where everything is known and clear, with the goal of learning and advancing to a new level in their career. After a while, they receive offers for positions along the same path, meaning the same duties they performed before. The income is not much, but still, it's money. So, the question is: is this a provocation aimed at throwing the person off course, or, on the other hand, are the gods helping, seeing that the person is not on the "right" path and is left without work?

Yllymakh: There are two types of provocation:

1. Destruction of everything: if you want to survive, adapt, look for working algorithms, or prove that your algorithms work and can save you.

2. A very sweet candy, in other words — temptation. You were tempted, you gave in, and then things went downhill…

Nobody likes provocation; you have to be a complete perverted masochist to enjoy such things. The goal of provocations is to make you find a working, that is, effective, action algorithm, remove the non-working one, or confirm that the algorithm you found really works. In short, provocation is war. It may be in micro-measurements, but it is still a war. The old will either be destroyed and make way for the new, or it will stand firm and destroy the new. The winner is the one who survives.

So judge for yourself — you chose a new path, a new algorithm, and it's difficult to follow. Immediately, a provocation in the form of temptation appears, testing the strength of the new algorithm. Then, if you hold firm, something else may come and begin to ruin your life. If the algorithm is effective, it will eliminate the obstacle and restore everything. If not — it will collapse itself.

Voislava: I've been in an endless financial crisis for several years now, but before, money came to me easily and in large amounts. Just before my situation worsened, I worked at a very good organization, where I liked everything, I was in my place, and I worked very effectively. In fact, the whole company depended on me. Then suddenly I was "laid off." Even then, I understood that my boss was afraid I might aim for her position, that I'd be promoted for my success, and she would be removed, so she preemptively struck. Only now do I realize I could have fought for myself. I could have gone to the board, even filed a lawsuit... I don't know if I would have worked at that company afterward, but the court would definitely have been on my side — 100%. Everything was official, every deal had a manager's signature attached, and they would have seen that I brought in most of the company's income, so "laying me off" was nonsense. But I didn't fight. I left proudly. And since then, money has turned its back on me. Before that situation, there was at least one other time when I resigned, and the company still owed me a lot of money. I accepted that I would never get it back and didn't fight for it. When I spoke to the former director, I didn't even bring it up. Now it's clear to me that this is how I gave up my right to that money. Please correct me if I'm thinking in the wrong direction.

Anna: Voislava, good afternoon. I've noticed such a law, or maybe it's not a law, I'm not sure. When they give, but I don't take — complete collapse follows. From this, I conclude (I learned from the runes) that I don't know how to take. Giving comes easily but taking… that's a problem. And if I refuse, the universe decides (I'm joking) that I don't need anything and takes the last bit from me. Of course, I make the decisions. It's not easy to fight for what's mine, but if necessary, I wouldn't hesitate to "tear the throat" of anyone who stands in my way. "Either me, or them. The strongest survives" — this phrase of Ksenia Evgenievna has become like an invisible seal, etched in my consciousness.

Gray Shaman: Good day to all. I'm reading this topic, and the sharpness of the moment is beginning to hit me. About 30 years ago, I came up with the idea to start a business with my father-in-law. Because of his mistakes, we had a falling out, my wife sided with her father — "give the money to dad…" I gave him the money, but during the time of maximum stress, I made a vow to myself: this woman, while she's with me, will never be wealthy. That's how we've been living… A question to the experts — have I lost any rights? I won't call us poor either.

Anna: Here's the answer for you. You set the program yourself, and it's being executed. It doesn't mention rights here. Who exactly did you want to prove something to back then?

Gray Shaman: It was a long time ago, and it's hard for me to say who or what I was trying to prove. But I remember this moment periodically. Most likely, this will be the first program which action I will stop as soon as I learn how to do that. My woman deserves more. At the time, I didn't trade her for a diamond mine — that was an offer.

Menshikova: You haven't lost your rights, you've blocked them. Now, there are two obvious options for you. The first: make it so that your beloved woman is not with you, if you prioritize her well-being over your own feelings. The second: take a counter-vow, which somewhat neutralizes the previous one — a conscious geis[11] that should somehow be linked to family or ancestral business as compensation for an incorrect action.

Phenix: Regarding voluntary surrender of rights, I highly recommend watching the film *"The Fox Hunter"*. It vividly shows the castes of rulers, merchants, and warriors. The betrayal of one's own caste and the transition to another level. The film's ending is explosive.

---

[11] For a detailed explanation of the system of geis, refer to Addendum 2 at the end of the book.

The director is clearly "in the know." It received an Oscar and many other awards at various festivals.

Ruta: Good day. I've decided that my question might be connected to the surrender of rights. The question is about altruism, time as a value, and who the weak are, to whom one should not help. A situation from real life: Two businessman clients reached out for a service (the essence of the service is not really important, but they really need it). One of them is successful but counts every penny and bargains down to the last, and it's unpleasant. The other is in a bad situation, owes money, but without the service, he'll be in even worse shape. At the same time, the majority of the clients are quite capable of paying, and everything is fine with them (this is to say that there's no special need to hold onto every client, but currently, there are no funds for charity). By the way, these two clients have been using the service for a long time, not just newcomers.

Clearly, with the first client, it's not about altruism, it's a matter of who gets the better of whom, but in response to his request for a discount, I just want to tell him to go away. The question is, should I offer the service to the second client, considering the real possibility that I may not get paid? Here on the forum, the rule of natural selection is often mentioned, but it's easy to talk about strangers and general situations, yet here we have communication that's been going on for about ten years. I'm not even talking about situations with closer people.

There's a fable by Robert Louis Stevenson: Once a sick person remained in a burning house when the fireman arrived.

"Don't save me," said the sick person, "save the strong."

"Please explain," said the fireman, since he was a polite man.

"It's the most honest thing to do," said the sick person. "The strong should be given preference in all circumstances because they can do more for our world."

The fireman thought for a moment because he was a person with a philosophical disposition.

"I agree," he finally said when the roof started to collapse. "But for the sake of continuing the conversation, tell me, what do you consider suitable work for the strong?"

"Nothing easier," responded the sick person. "The right work for the strong is helping the weak."
The fireman thought again, since there was no rush for this remarkable creature.

"I can forgive you for being sick," he said at last, as part of the wall collapsed, "but I certainly can't tolerate that you're such a fool."

With these words, he raised his axe and with one precise blow pinned the sick person to the bed.

For some reason, I often attract people who need help, and now I'm starting to think about each situation, but I can't find the line where I should refuse. How is altruism defined in magic, and is it always harmful? How does the warrior caste determine for itself the concept of help and situations where it's possible? Can you share your point of view?

Deva Soma: From what I'm familiar with and what I remember from my training, I can say that, firstly, as long as you don't realize your own value, there will always be people around you trying to "chip off a piece" from you — whether it's your time, energy, territory, or some other resource. And secondly, help should only be given in situations where a person truly cannot handle things on their own. You cannot take away someone's experience; this may be necessary for some kind of personal processing for that person. I remember that during one of the training seminars, we were asked to think about why "good" people die young, for example. That is, you can point out the brick wall that is in the person's way, and where to unload it, but you cannot do it for them. There's also the possibility that you might twist each other's karma, and then you'll have to meet in the next life if you don't work it out in this one. This especially applies to healers. When they heal just for the sake of healing, they might not be able to reincarnate after death and ascend to a higher realm, having accumulated too many "debtors." Whether to help or not — no one can intuitively guide you on this.

Olga_: Colleagues and teachers, I have a question: is my situation a voluntary renunciation of rights?

The situation: my mother's unexpected death seven years ago (I was in a state of apathy and depression with two young children). My father and brother and I meet at the notary's office regarding the inheritance. My mother, as I thought, had nothing but a car, a garage, and a small amount of money on her card. During the meeting, my father (who had provided me with everything I needed: housing, education) told me that I should renounce the inheritance, just as he did, in favor of my brother. I felt a tightening inside, and my father said, "Don't worry, it's just a formality, since your brother is a lawyer, he'll handle everything fairly, and we won't need to run around to all the agencies." At the time, I had no knowledge of the inheritance procedure. In complete trust, with love for my father, I signed the renunciation.

As a result, seven years after my mother's death, it turned out that she owned 1/2 of all of my father's property, which was acquired together. And this includes a lot: houses, land, apartments, real estate, business assets. I just found out now that all of this belongs to my brother. I was cleverly isolated, as there was always disobedience, uncontrollability, and an element of chaos within me (they couldn't control me honestly). I was deceived by love.

Is trust and ignorance of one's rights considered a VOLUNTARY RENUNCIATION OF THEM? Thank you in advance.

Ekaterina NM: It is considered so. Ignorance does not absolve you from responsibility. Though it's not entirely clear what ignorance you're referring to, you voluntarily, not just verbally but in writing, signed documents renouncing the inheritance — everything is more than transparent. You believed your mother's inheritance was small, but even a small inheritance is still a resource. What motivated you to renounce it? Love? That's a questionable explanation. Love is acceptance of everything, both the small and the large.

From your explanation, it's evident that you didn't want to make an effort to fill out the documents. Your father and brother used their mental and causal realm[12] — they thought and planned the sequence of events, while you were in emotions at the astral level. This is clearly an indicator of the difference in the level of your consciousness and theirs. Your consciousness was at a lower level.

Can you get your rights back? It's unlikely. After all, inheritance is not just material things, as you've

---

[12] Mental and causal bodies — the spheres of thinking and experience, respectively. Higher spheres of thinking, in contrast to, for example, emotions and sensations. In this case, the colleague points out that the opponents in this matter were in higher positions of consciousness, which ultimately determined their victory.

described. Inheritance is something more: currents, rights, information — you voluntarily gave all of this to your brother. You can only get it back if your brother also voluntarily returns it.

Milena: Hello, colleagues! I have the following question: At one point, Ksenia Evgenievna mentioned in a lecture that a war veteran loses rights when asking for a seat on public transport or to bypass the queue at the clinic. But what about actors who appear in advertisements for banks, cosmetics, and the like? They are selling their name for money, right? In this case, are they voluntarily giving up their rights to the merchant caste? Am I understanding this correctly that models, whose "bread" is to appear in advertisements, just keep growing with every new offer, while actors, athletes, writers, and scientists lose?

Yllymakh: Actors themselves belong to the merchant caste. Changing capital in the merchant caste is normal, even an obligation. For some, the capital is sympathies, for others, it's money. The exchange is mutually beneficial, within the caste. There are no losses.

Milena: Yllymakh, thank you. It never occurred to me that actors are merchants. But it's true, the newer generation of them — all at corporate events and in TV shows, grabbing onto any "gig." It's so sad sometimes to see their wrinkled faces on billboards for some pharmacy.

I was once friends with the daughter of a well-known director. He's no longer in demand and now shoots TV shows he doesn't even want to make. By the way, the fees for directors of TV series on federal channels are quite decent. I'm trying to understand — a person who devoted their whole life to their craft, a fanatic, at the twilight of their fame, steps on their own principles.

Nadezhda Voronina: I think the question is more subtly formulated. For example, I was disturbed by a recent story about how a Soviet athlete, who won Olympic medals as a young girl (a warrior at the time, undoubtedly), sold her medals at an auction (a location of merchants).

There's such cognitive dissonance from this story that I can't explain. And it's not even about the price, although it seems they paid her quite a lot. It's the fact of selling something that you earned with sweat and blood for money.

Wayfarer: Nadezhda Voronina, what exactly bothers you? That the warrior exchanged their victory prize for money? Well, they gave him a reward in medals instead of money, what's the issue? We don't know what prompted the person to act this way: an impossible situation, a serious illness... Who knows? What if it was psychologically easier for her to sell (not personally, mind you, but through specialists in this field) her well-earned medals than to publicly beg the powerful of the world on TV, telling heartbreaking stories about her extreme need?

Let's look at this situation from another angle: yes, the victory was the goal at the time, now it's a fact, it is what it is, and the reward (the pleasant bonus that accompanied the victory) — is it a value or a tool? We live for values (do we live for medals?), we achieve goals and use tools to achieve those goals. Logically, if it's a tool, then why not monetize this resource when necessary?

Milena: Wayfarer, in my opinion, the medal is not just a piece of gold; it's blood, sweat, tears, iron will, a ton of limitations, insane belief in victory, and time (a lot of time!). By selling it, you're selling all of that for money, bulk selling it, so to speak, thus leveling it out.

Wayfarer: Milena, it's true that there's a certain loss of existential volume. I would have said six months ago that the medal is sweat, blood, and tears. Now I think this: victory is the achieved goal. The victory itself wasn't sold. The medal is just an item, no matter how you look at it. What it symbolizes for the owner is known only to the owner. I think an Olympic champion wouldn't just part with it easily, there must be a serious reason, and we don't know that reason. But if such a situation arose, it's hard to say definitively that selling the medal equals a loss of rights or a transition to a lower caste. What if they need money for treating their children or grandchildren from cancer, for example? To proudly gaze at their sweat, blood, and tears embodied in a golden disk? Seriously, there are different situations.

I would like to know the opinion of the senior colleagues on this matter.

Nadezhda Voronina: Wayfarer, in that case, it seems we need to understand what exact condition she laid down when selling her medals. If she said, "I'm selling my victory along with these medals," that's one thing. If she said, "I'm selling a piece of metal," that's something else. In that case, the merchants would be the fools because they'd be buying wrappers.

Wayfarer: Nadezhda Voronina, of course. This is primarily a question of her goals and values. After all, if she says, "The medal is my victory, I can't sell it," she loses an additional tool for solving other problems... But if she sells it out of despair, then it's a loss of rights and so on.

The merchants are not fools, they're in their place, and they bought a valuable collectible item. She sold that item because she considered it necessary for herself.

Yllymakh: Regarding the medals. My grandfather returned from the war with a bunch of medals. He immediately gave them to his younger brothers and sisters to play with. He didn't care about their fate later. He didn't like the ceremonial costumes with medals worn by other veterans. He called the medals "trinkets" and veterans adorned with them "Christmas trees." He had contempt for any show-off. So, I think you're right — a medal is nothing more than an object, a symbol. The idea that with the sale of the medal, the winner sold their victory, could only have come from a merchant. Because they have no idea what victory is, and measure everything in money. Don't confuse surrendering rights with pulling resources. Every higher caste has the right to pull resources from a lower caste without losing anything for themselves. Loss only occurs when the motivation behind the action does not align with your own caste but corresponds to the motivation of a lower caste.

Nadezhda Voronina: A merchant wouldn't even think about that. Exactly, "because they have no idea what victory is, and measure everything in money." That's what this whole conversation was meant to highlight — to clarify the kinds of misunderstandings, to understand how to behave properly in various situations. And indeed, situations are truly different. Even Ksenia Evgenievna says that merchants are now surpassing warriors. Many can't handle it and "sell out." The loss of rights by one warrior weakens the entire caste. So, there is cause for concern, and such precedents exist. They are not rare. Who knows, what formulation did she use when selling the medals? Perhaps this can be tracked by the future fate of the athlete. If she enters a "zone of cataclysms," then it means the formulation was wrong. I just thought about it — assigning labels, which caste's path does that belong to?

Yllymakh: "Just thought about it — assigning labels, which caste's path does that belong to?" The one that doesn't think. Stereotypes are a product of collective, not individual, mind. That's the laborers.

Clarissa: Colleagues, how do you distinguish collective thinking from non-collective thinking? If it's not collective, then what kind of thinking is it? What in our minds is more or less our own, rather than assimilated, absorbed, or adapted from some sources? Well, we don't eat oatmeal for breakfast in kindergarten with everyone; we eat what our mom made. A question of minority/majority, but hardly of uniqueness.

Menshikova: In the collective, it's always safe. Staying in the mental field of the majority calms and gives (so to speak) a background feeling of personal significance. It may not even identify itself as an independent feeling, but it acts as a catalyst for any other feelings related to safety ("everything is correct").

Individual thinking has the opposite characteristics and results in opposite effects. It's scary. It's terrifying. It vibrates. It excites the awareness of inner freedom, but damn, it's scary. You'll see the effects.

As for the lady who sold her medals. Well, really, what's the big deal? She traded metal junk for other junk, more useful. Truly. But. What are medals for victory? They are symbols of victory. Victory is an immaterial thing. In the material world, it has a reflection — the medal. If you get rid of the symbol, you get rid of what it symbolized. So, the lady lost her victory. And she exchanged her right to it for money.

As colleagues have well noted, her victory was valued strictly at market price — that is, by the merchants. Now and for a long time, the price of her achievements will depend on the merchant's opinion — that's one; it won't be counted as a victory until the merchants allow it — that's two.

This, as you understand, applies to any victory, not just athletic achievements, which certainly won't happen now.

Nadezhda Voronina: Thank you, Ksenia Evgenievna. So, it wasn't for nothing that the cats were scratching. By the way, there's a long backstory to this. This athlete was offered by merchants from abroad to buy her medals for a large sum back in the USSR. At that time, it was unthinkable. But they planted the seed of doubt. And now it's grown. Thank you also for the explanation about collective thinking. It really helps to understand things better.

Voislava: "For example, I was disturbed by the recent story about how a Soviet athlete, who won Olympic medals as a girl (for me, undoubtedly a warrior at that time), sold her medals at an auction (the location of merchants)."

She also accused her coach of sexually abusing her during the Olympics. If the act is mercantile, then the merchant here represents their worst qualities: by doing nothing specific, just talking, they stir up interest in themselves, sympathy, so they can get something out of it for themselves, while devaluing the coach decades after their shared victories.

Lecz: Good day, everyone! If we talk about the case of selling the medals (may Olga forgive us), I believe that in this case, no rights were sold. Medals are just attributes that confirm those rights. She earned the right to be a world champion through her performances. Medals are the result of those performances. The law of cause and effect.

If you remove the physical proof of this effect in the form of sold awards, does the cause lose its meaning as such? Probably not. She was and remains the world champion for millions of people. You could also consider the example of emigrating aristocrats during difficult times, forced to sell their family treasures and orders to survive. Did they become commoners afterward, and did those who bought these orders become aristocrats? I don't think so. Rights are still an inner state, not a manifestation of material things.

Natalika: "Rights are still an inner state, not a manifestation of material things."
Perhaps, there's still a difference in what kind of material we're talking about. If it's some objects or real estate bought with money that accompanied the rights, that's one thing. But medals are symbols of the right itself. In my opinion, selling symbols nullifies the rights, as it involves exchanging the right for money. After all, they don't pay for the badge, but for the symbol of the right.

Voislava: I think so too. I read about Vivien Leigh, and how she treated her Oscars quite dismissively. One, she even propped a door with, another was almost standing in the bathroom. But she didn't auction them off, waiting to see who would offer the most money for them.
It's the same with veterans' awards. If they don't wear them and don't particularly treasure them, it doesn't diminish their feats. But if they sell their awards (though I haven't heard of veterans doing this themselves — usually, it's their descendants), it's a whole different matter. The feats, of course, don't go anywhere. The rights do.

Nadezhda Voronina: Here's something else that came to mind. My grandmother buried my grandfather's military medals with him. She regretted it for a long time. She said they could have been sold for a lot of money. But what's done is done. It seems this act preserved my grandfather's right to victory. It's amazing how life unfolds.

THE CASTE SYSTEM
OF THIS WORLD

The human world is divided into caste-based societies, and this is the law of the present moment. Castes can be officially defined within a system of relations, but in most cases, this phenomenon exists informally. However, the omission of certain aspects of life is not a valid reason to declare their absence; it only exacerbates the problem of ignorance.

Castes are not criteria of social inequality. Castes are a conditional classification of people based on:
- Needs;
- Abilities;
- Psychological and physiological characteristics. And, as a result, missions for each individual in a particular incarnation.

Legends and myths that tell us how the gods determined the castes of the human world are varied, numerous, and rich in significant and less significant details. From all these legends, three key elements can be deduced.

First: the algorithm for assigning a human society to a particular caste periodically changes, but for each such algorithm, a certain and non-redundant period of time is given for its development.

Second: the division into four castes remains unchanged— laborers, merchants, warriors, and rulers. In fact, it is customary to highlight a fifth caste of mages, but since mages are not fully related to the human world, defining their community alongside human systems and assigning them to the fifth caste is not always justified or appropriate.

Third: castes are necessary for the evolution of human consciousness from a primitive being to a god. Therefore, it is impossible to skip levels— a laborer cannot become a warrior without first becoming a merchant.

The criteria for assigning consciousness to a particular caste, as already mentioned, periodically change, and this is a systemic mechanism. The requirements for passing through levels are an algorithm that is constantly becoming more complex.

Now, in more detail.

Each person is born and undergoes initial formation within a certain caste. From the perspective of the algorithmic formation of castes, each caste includes people and minimal human societies (such as the family), based on the magnitude of the existential volume (EV) of consciousness. For each caste, this is a set magnitude and represents a conditional range. The collective consciousness of all people within a particular caste must represent a complete unity—a single entity. Moreover, for each of the four castes, the specific value of this unity is different. This is the programming mathematics.

Existential volume is the cumulative experience accumulated by the soul and consciousness throughout life. Experience is not memory. Experience can be reflected in memory, but it may not be. Experience consists of algorithms for achieving results, programs that take into account both survival and success in different specific times and spaces.

Experience is universal if the algorithm for achieving results in all lands and at all times not only helps survival but also leads to success. Experience is specific (limited) if it allows survival and victory only in certain spaces, times, or circumstances. It is clear that the indicator of universality or specificity also affects the final value of the existential volume of consciousness.

It can be said that the original goal of human incarnation is to conduct field tests of various or specific algorithms for achieving results, checking them for their ability to function in any software environment. This includes even such a viral and limiting one as the current one.

A human's "entry" into a particular caste depends on two factors—the magnitude of the existential volume (EV) of the consciousness, formed through previous incarnations (the EV of the soul), and the EV of the blood—the family into which one happens to be born.

The old algorithm, which existed not so long ago (approximately until the year 1000 AD), did not allow the EV of the soul to be lower than the EV of the blood.

Therefore, it was utterly unlikely for a merchant to be born into a family of rulers or for a warrior to be born into a family of laborers. However, after certain manipulations with the reprogramming of the egregorial space, these rules were abolished, and what we see now represents a complete eclecticism, allowing merchants to have a child who becomes a ruler and warriors to raise a son who becomes a merchant. A significant role in the abolishment of this rule was played by the acceptance of morganatic marriages—incest that violates the rules of caste[13]. A lower caste can use the laws of union with a higher caste without any harm to itself, but if a higher caste adheres to the rules of the lower caste, the harm caused by such a connection becomes evident very quickly—up to the complete degeneration of the bloodline.

A person's personal EV, according to the old algorithm, was justly calculated as the weighted average of the soul's EV and the blood's EV. However, when mass violations of the old blood-union rule began, the gap between the EV of the soul and the EV of the blood could become immense, and this started happening more and more frequently. The Abrahamic religions, which by this time had become firmly established in the egregorial program world as highly influential players (and in many lands, even the only players), solved this problem

---

[13] Each caste has its own rules for marriage and the birth of children. The rules suitable for laborers are in no way appropriate for warriors, and the allowances possible in merchant families could destroy the caste of rulers.

elegantly, simply, and not without significant benefit for themselves: the EV of a person's identity began to be determined by the lowest indicator. A higher indicator (whether of the soul or the blood) was programmatically reduced (especially since by this time all the mechanisms for such reduction had already been developed: rituals of purification, repentance, the institution of sinfulness, and most importantly, the institution of slavery). Without spiritual slavery, it would have been very difficult to carry out this plan, since according to unbreakable laws, rights—many of which are determined by the person's EV—can only be given away voluntarily. But if someone needs to be nullified, it is better if this can be done automatically—the person must be born a slave (Judaism), dedicated to slavery immediately after birth (Christianity), or become a slave by their own will or the will of their parents (Islam).

Thus, the criteria for belonging to a particular caste are now in the hands of religious (occasionally governmental and/or authoritative) systems, which possess a well-established and highly refined mechanism for increasing or decreasing a person's EV.

However, personal memory, when freed from slave affiliation, has the ability to restore its highest EV values. This ability is reflected in consciousness as long-term memory.

Long-term memory manifests in the continuity between lives. There is, however, a distinction in the effects of the manifestation of the long-term memory of the soul or the long-term memory of the blood.

The long-term memory of the soul is the continuity of EV accumulation from one incarnation to the next. EV does not diminish at the moment of death and completely transitions into the new life. This is possible only when a person, at the moment of transition, does not voluntarily renounce their experience (repentance), does not allow others to assess their experience by foreign standards (spiritual circumcision, sanctification, collective judgment, etc.). In this case, their experience is not truncated, does not transition from slave to master, and consciousness and memory are not reset like an old computer prepared for resale.

The long-term memory of the soul manifests both in specific memories and simply as knowledge (people call it wisdom). In magical training, it is believed that it is this long-term memory that forms the fundamental basis for the development of consciousness in magic and for breaking free from the inevitable programmatic membership in the human caste system.

The long-term memory of blood is the continuity of EV accumulation within a single bloodline, within one family. This line can be interrupted through magical rituals of renunciation, which occur during initiation into monastic life, as well as through committing crimes like patricide[14]. In all other cases, the EV of blood is very difficult to diminish or extract, as the right to power through blood is an ancient tradition, originating from the historical depths of the birth of the gods, and it is under the authority of the Mother, of the Earth, and of nature. The long-term memory of blood manifests as the continuous memories (experience) of blood relatives. It is believed that the presence of long-term memory of blood is essential for belonging to the caste of rulers.

A bit about the castes themselves.

The first caste is the caste of laborers. This is the most numerous caste in terms of its composition. Representatives of this caste seek settledness and stability. They are primarily oriented around biological rhythms—life and death, sleep and wakefulness. The mechanism for managing this caste is based on basic emotions, the fear of death, and the need for safety in life.

The characteristic of existence within this caste is inertia. The consciousness of people belonging to it is unable to perceive an idea as an idea; it can only understand rules. Not even laws, as generalized conditions of existence, but only rules. Commandments. Without ambiguity, and the simpler, the better. People of

---

[14] More precisely, any older relative with whom the murderer is connected by a single bloodline. Currently, this includes not only direct connections but also indirect ones: slander, defamation, negligence, insult—any action that could lead to the harm of an older relative of any gender.

the laborer caste are religious, but not out of faith, rather out of fear. They are capable of trust, but not of belief, and prefer to equate these concepts rather than distinguish between them. They do not like changing their place of residence and strive to take root as deeply as possible anywhere, regardless of losses or harm. Natural selection manifests here in the principle of survival. The criterion for evaluating success is survival.

The second caste is the caste of merchants. It is significantly smaller in number than the caste of laborers, but still quite considerable. Compared to the caste of laborers, merchants are more mobile, but they still tend to gravitate towards a certain stability. For laborers, stability is important today, while the warrior caste is oriented towards stability tomorrow.

This caste is governed by higher emotions, such as love and hatred. These emotions, in contrast to the basic emotions of the fear of death and the need for safety, are more prolonged in time and are remembered for longer. This is a significant difference in the psychology of laborers and merchants: the feelings of merchants are more complex and long-term.

Merchants have the ability to manage the caste of laborers. Unlike the latter, the consciousness of merchants is not only capable of perceiving an idea as an idea but also of forming various rules based on that idea. However, they cannot grasp the global meaning of the idea; they will never see the philosophical component of the idea and prefer to operate with the term "law" rather than "meaning." Because law is something clear. They depend on the law, and at this level of consciousness, they learn not only to obey it but also to at least attempt to understand it.

In the merchant caste, the primary algorithms of management are developed. One could say that this is the testing environment for the development of the qualities of power, with the caste of laborers serving as the subject.

At this level, the principle of natural selection operates not so much on the level of physical survival as it does on the basis of victory in the battle of characters: who is faster, who is more insightful, who is bolder, who is more skilled, and so on. Here, the criterion for evaluating success is the maximum number of connections a merchant can establish during their existence in the caste.

However, for a further transition into the warrior caste, these connections must collapse in such a way that quantity turns into quality and determines the purpose of these connections.

The third caste is the caste of warriors. It is fewer in number compared to the previous two castes and is even more mobile. Management of this caste is not done on the level of emotions and feelings, but at the level of higher mental states: faith, duty, service, purity of thought. The characteristic feature of the consciousness of this caste is long memory.

The transition from the merchant level to the warrior level occurs when a person begins to ask themselves the question "why?". At this level, consciousness begins to work not with rules or laws. Here, people learn to deal with meanings.

This is why this caste is called the caste of warriors: only a warrior can subdue their instincts for the sake of a goal; only a warrior can disregard personal feelings for the sake of meaning; only a warrior can forsake obvious benefit for the sake of a non-obvious benefit.

The transition from caste to caste rarely happens within one lifetime; it usually occurs during the transition to the next incarnation. This is merciful for the psyche and painless for the body, as the experience of such a transition in a state of awareness is very painful, agonizingly unbearable, and is punished by severe depression. However, if a person is capable of such a transition, survives, and remains in sound mind, their EV can be increased by a significant coefficient immediately.

For a warrior, the question "why?" is of primary importance. The questions "how?" and "how much?" should remain at the levels of the laborer and merchant castes, respectively.

Wealth and the ability to show oneself are not priorities for a warrior. A warrior may be wealthy, or they may not be. What matters to a warrior is being devoted to their cause. A doctor who is devoted to their profession and continues to heal despite everything is a warrior, whereas one who provides medical services is a merchant. A scholar who is devoted to their subject is a warrior, while one who changes their focus because another topic offers a large grant is a merchant. Money for a warrior is a test, just as fear of the law is for a merchant. A warrior is not afraid of the law because they understand its meaning. However, the formation in the warrior caste must not only teach those undergoing this transformation all the algorithms of resilience and loyalty but also shape the correct experience of managing the merchant caste so that the test of poverty becomes a past trial successfully completed.

If a warrior, who besides developing the right properties of consciousness also forms the correct mechanisms of influence for those who acquire resources (on merchants and, through them, on laborers), then their path to the caste of rulers will be open. The entry ticket here is not only understanding the principle and idea of the victory of their god (that is, themselves in human projection) but also implementing this principle in the management of the merchant caste. The result here is ensuring all the needs of oneself and their interests in such a way that the merchant caste itself will desire to create laws for itself based on this victorious principle. They must want such power and, for it, willingly give up everything this caste possesses.

The fourth caste is the caste of rulers. It is minimal in number. The mechanism of governance is impeccability.

To preemptively eliminate any cognitive dissonance from readers, let me clarify the following. The one who is currently called a ruler, from the perspective of the other castes, is unlikely to be considered such according to the ideal and originally conceived definition. However, the magical perspective on the issue does not see any violation of the rule here—because the programmatic filling with algorithms, which belongs to each caste today, is no longer done by gods; it is done by Abrahamic religions. They are free to put their own concepts into the idea of "impeccability," which are very different from the parameters that were formed when people lived with their gods without any egregors. And there is no need to refer to courtly literature about chivalry and valor—while it emerged during the monotheistic period, it is entirely a projection of old pagan traditions.

Similarly, the Abrahamic system has also substituted its own definitions for concepts such as "honor," "valor," "righteousness," "order," and "benefit." It even managed to adapt "safety" for its own needs, although biology is the area where artificial systems find it hardest to exert influence.

The transition to the caste of rulers cannot happen during life, unlike the previous transitions from the laborer caste to the merchant caste and from the merchant caste to the warrior caste. It cannot, primarily, because here, blood plays a role, not just spirit. This means that one must be born into a specific bloodline, and the blood must accept the person and enrich their EV with its informational strength.

In Roman mythology, there are special guardian spirits of the bloodline—numina. The primary task of the numen's program is to ensure the continuous bloodline, to ensure generational continuity, which will guarantee the descendants' long-term memory and, through it, the constant growth of EV through blood. The numen was meant to protect the family—not just the lives of the descendants but also to safeguard them from reckless actions that would suggest an unwise descendant had voluntarily renounced their rights to the bloodline. This was important because Roman civilization formed all the algorithms of the institution of power, the results of which we are fortunate enough to witness in today's world—the offspring of Roman civilization[15].

Among the Celts, such a tribal spirit-program was called the Banshee, and among the Slavs, it was called the *Bereginya*.

✼ ✼ ✼

---

[15] Those who are well-versed in Roman history, especially after Emperor Augustus, will not be surprised that the institution of power turned out the way it did. Everything is logical.

As already mentioned, one can only reach the higher castes by fully undergoing the formation in each caste. And why is that? Because at each level, one must take and work through all the experience that the caste has accumulated by the time of incarnation. And not just work through it, but also apply it to one's personal algorithm of victory and survival[16], complicate it under new temporal and spatial circumstances, making oneself and one's algorithm informationally invulnerable. This process takes time. And the longer humanity lives, the more informationally rich it becomes from century to century, the faster the consciousness of one undergoing this formation must be to keep up with everything and not lose what has been achieved. Loss ensures a quick return to the laborer caste with the suggestion to start over.

The warrior caste, unlike the merchant caste and, of course, the laborer caste, possesses a rather specific right to property. By nature, warriors cannot be sedentary, they cannot have much property—the right to own something is determined only by the amount they are able to carry with them, to take on their person. Any other property burdens them, ties them down, including the need for a settled life, which is categorically unacceptable in the warrior caste. If a warrior begins to

---

[16] More precisely, the algorithm of your god, with whom you are essentially one.

accumulate property, they will soon turn into a merchant, if not a laborer.

To avoid any illusions about one's own rights, it must be stated that the true right to land in the caste world of humans belongs only to the members of the ruler caste. This right of ownership was established a long time ago, when the principles of the transfer of royal power were formed in the civilization of the Irish Celts. A true ruler is one who is "married" to the Earth. All others only have the right to use it, and this right is never hereditary for laborers, merchants, or warriors—only for rulers. The piece of paper that secures the "right to land" is a fiction, an illusion created in the human world, and has nothing to do with true rights.

When a person transitions into the warrior caste, they form a rather specific relationship to time—it becomes a value. And the longer a warrior stays in the informational space of their caste, the more time becomes the main measure of the effectiveness of life and activity. Not money. Not power. Not relationships. Not knowledge. Time.

When the understanding of changed values comes, a warrior can no longer sell their time for money. Knowledge—perhaps, skills—perhaps, but not time. Therefore, a warrior, if they recognize themselves as such, will never work "by schedule," giving away their legitimate eight hours to a merchant. This is unacceptable; it diminishes the warrior in their own eyes and severely undermines the rights of their caste—a warrior does not sell their time for money; this is the law. And if circumstances arise such that they are forced to work for a merchant, then the warrior, if they truly are a warrior, must ensure that over time, things will shift—eventually, the merchant will truly serve the warrior, follow their instructions, and depend on them. Although formally, the merchant may still be considered the master.

To avoid any illusions among the readers that a warrior by caste must necessarily be a warrior by profession or social position, let me state clearly—this is not the case. The realities of today, the law, and "democracy" allow that high positions are now occupied by merchants—both officials and internal defenders, and some scholars, and people of science—there are many merchants in positions where they do not belong. This is not a flaw in the system; it is the defeat of the warrior caste by the merchant caste. It is not final yet, everything can be corrected, but the fact remains: warriors voluntarily lose their caste positions, becoming merchants when the main value shifts from time to money and connections. In this case, they exchange one for the other, not even realizing how, in an instant, they lose the positions they worked so hard to gain.

Recently, quite a few women have been born into the warrior caste. In this case, it is a natural reaction of the caste to the forced losses suffered at the hands of the merchant caste: women have proven to be physically and psychologically more resilient, and more faithful to their commitments, as recent catastrophes have shown. But life in a patriarchal society, and consequently, adherence to all patriarchal laws, imposes on a woman-warrior the obligation to acquire the proper skills for the caste. Namely:

- To choose a husband wisely. At the very least, someone from her own caste. The rule of the patriarchal world, "the slave becomes a slave by following the slave," has not been abolished;
- To accept her solitude if she cannot unite her fate with a member of her own caste, rather than marry just anyone;
- To prove, at this level, that she can manage her own time without relying on the rules of patriarchal society.

The affirmation of women in the warrior caste is currently an experiment. The conditions for its success are difficult, but the game is worth the candle.

* * *

It is always easier to fall to a lower level than to rise back up. The law states: the higher a person rises in the caste hierarchy, the more frequent and harsh the provocations will be, testing their right to be in that position. The trial of merchantism is also a provocation. And very few have withstood it. The descendants of the victorious warrior could not retain the right to victory, breaking under the trial of great wealth. As it turned out, enduring poverty, deprivation, and powerlessness is easier than enduring abundance, wealth, and freedom.

Let us hope that the next generation of the warrior caste, mainly composed of women, will be able to reclaim lost positions and strengthen the power of their caste. And the most important lesson that new warriors must learn from the previous losses is this: never, under any circumstances, sell your time for money.

Time is the price of any striving game: whoever has a reserve of time also holds the right to the future.

The described algorithm for building a caste society is the algorithm of today. No one says it will shape the future—not at all. The future will be shaped by other algorithms (which will be discussed in other books and relate more to the line of mages than humans). But this future will not arrive until the current project is brought to its logical conclusion, and the best principles of survival and victory are defined, which will then be enshrined in law to form the program of the upcoming reality. Or rather—realities.

Iryna: So, if our offender is stronger energetically, do we still have the right to revenge, regardless of the inequality of forces?

Menshikova: Energy has absolutely nothing to do with it. It all depends on the level of rights—the higher the caste, the greater the rights. Including the right to vengeance.

Example: If a laborer offends a merchant, the merchant has the right to demand satisfaction according to the degree of the offense and the "rates" for such offenses in the merchant caste. But if a merchant offends a laborer, the laborer has no legal right to anything. The only way to compensate for the damage (the offense) is to go to the witch. And she knows how to circumvent this law.

But a warrior should remember the following. As the ancient law of the warrior-mage states: "If something or someone harms or threatens you, your life, your loved ones, your rights, or your well-being, it must be destroyed. Immediately." Deliberations on this subject lower the warrior beneath the merchant who offended them.

Therefore, it would be beneficial if everyone could honestly and without illusions determine their caste position. In this case, there will be no issues with determining the caste of the person opposite.

M: Thank you! Ksenia Evgenievna, where can I read more about the laws for castes, the laws of our world? I have to gather it piece by piece from your lectures. Perhaps there is some information in literature form? Or do you cover this in the theory of magic?

Menshikova: In magical studies, essential information often has to be gathered piece by piece. Which is generally not difficult if you have two things in your arsenal: time and a search algorithm. Specifically, a book where everything is explained, with references to primary sources, commentary, and evidence—such a book I don't know. But the maximum information can be found in the library section on "Celtic Magic" on the website. Also (off the top of my head):
- The Salic Law;
- Irish sagas;
- The Scandinavian "Song of Rig";
- Chronicles of the Long-Haired Kings... In general, the library is your help.

Guest: Is there a connection between diseases and castes? In other words, do different castes suffer from different diseases?

Yllymakh: Personally, from my observations—yes, there is. I do not claim this as absolute truth, it's just what I've observed.

Laborers—frequent viral diseases, unsanitary conditions, bone diseases, and so on. Merchants—venereal diseases, infertility, alcoholism, drug addiction, obesity.

Warriors—often cerebral palsy, congenital defects, injuries, serious physical illnesses, absence of limbs and their defects, etc. In my impression, injuries are often a result of participation in wars, disputes, or criminal activities in past lives—so-called "beginning warriors."

Mages—mental disorders, intellectual disabilities, underdevelopment. Less frequently—drug addiction, gambling, alcoholism, but the key word here is mania. Even alcoholism here is of a different type.

I determine the caste by three directions: horoscopes, my own feelings from their energy, as I have more empathy than clairvoyance, and information about the observed person's family. I used to use cards—both playing and Tarot—but I am not using them for now.

Mila: So, does that mean the higher the caste, the more complicated the diseases?

Yllymakh: From my observations, the two upper castes do not get sick at all. All their diseases are the consequences of karmic programs or mistakes. Warriors more frequently get sick when they are beginners. Once they have established themselves in the caste and the family line moves steadily upward, illnesses are almost nonexistent. As a rule, the sick, especially among mages, are the scapegoats of the family. I attribute this to the increase in energetic potential in these castes, as well as to their proper behavior and the ability to correct karmic programs. For mages, healing and self-healing from very severe diseases, such as cancer, is normal. A warrior who breaks through can be considered a mage. Merchants with such an illness are practically doomed.

Natalia: Based on this logic, beginning warriors suffer injuries—"baptism of fire." As a test of endurance and the right to even be in this caste.

Yllymakh: It seems to me that this is the result of the first trials and errors in a new caste—when you don't yet know the rules, you try everything, and then you work through your own mistakes. It is more noticeable in the upper castes because they generally rarely get sick. In the lower castes, such transitional age difficulties likely also exist, but they are less noticeable due to the frequent health problems within the entire caste at any level.

Guest: Yllymakh, interesting observations. And the "epidemics" of the century—cardiovascular diseases, diabetes, osteochondrosis, Alzheimer's—what caste would you associate them with?

Yllymakh: I've been thinking about diabetes... Like other hormonal diseases, I haven't yet assigned it to any particular caste. I suspect these diseases are part of the transition from merchants to warriors. Among the people I've observed, diabetics are all warriors. Their lives are governed by strict rules: if you want to live, follow the regimen. Their willpower becomes as strong as reinforced concrete, especially in children.

I've never seen Alzheimer's. Hepatitis is common among merchants, stomach issues are common among warriors. I've seen heart conditions in both merchants and warriors, but only one case among mages. So, heart problems are still in question.

Among mages, I've seen provocations related to blood—malignant hypertension with "miraculous" self-healing, all kinds of vegetative-vascular dystonia, which people suffered from and then suddenly healed, and one case of HIV disappearance—the diagnosis was made, then it was removed, explained as errors, and this happened in several hospitals. Personally, I do not recognize HIV and VSD as standalone diseases—it seems more likely there's something wrong with the energy.

Marfa Vasilyevna: Greetings, colleagues. Regarding the issue of caste differences, we have indeed spoken little about the ruler caste, mostly describing the first three. This is likely because they are closer, more familiar, and more widely represented in the surrounding world as subjects for research. I've been long troubled by the question: what is the fundamental difference in consciousness between rulers and the other castes? Why are there so few rulers? What qualities of consciousness allow them not just to rule over others, but to influence the very foundation of their system—implementing their own values and beliefs, sometimes replacing one set of principles with another, which is essentially rewriting a program, demolishing the old system of another person? I would be grateful for any help in understanding this question.

I imagined the stages of consciousness evolution as a line, a kind of scale from zero to one, where 0 is an absolutely unstable, unstable system, most susceptible to change, and 1 is the most stable. From the consciousness of a laborer to the consciousness of a ruler. Reflecting on this image, I eventually came to a rather paradoxical conclusion: the more fixed a system is, the less stable it is, and vice versa. But this conclusion is only paradoxical from the first (human) perspective. In the end, what is the determining factor in evolution? The ability to change.

It would seem that in order to preserve its essence, it must be as clearly fixed as possible. This is the wall I hit several months ago when I was trying to understand how one could not betray the connection with their god in any way other than through priesthood. It is precisely the cynical lack of principle of the ruler that makes their system the most stable. But the cynicism and lack of principle, which irritate members of the other castes, is not the cause itself; it is only the reflection of it in the human world.

Perhaps this is why the ruler caste stands apart from the other three. The first three, despite their apparent differences, are actually very similar. Why do all three castes dislike the others? Why do the principles of the other castes often seem incomplete, primitive, unnatural, unworthy, and sometimes even cause disgust and condemnation? I'm not speaking in general terms, I'm speaking of the overwhelming majority of cases, of people who are not inclined to introspection.

The fewer principles and constants a person operates with, the more tightly they cling to them, the less they are able to change or add to them, the more fanatical and orthodox their views are, the more rigid and primitive their system of values and beliefs becomes. With each new step along this imagined scale from laborer to ruler, a person expands their system more and more, incorporating new algorithms and constants, becoming less susceptible to influence and forced change from the outside. They become more difficult to use for the purposes of representatives of higher castes. But what really distinguishes a ruler from the others, besides the fact that they have advanced the farthest on the path? I believe the main difference lies precisely in their apparent lack of principle, and essentially, in their ability to give equal weight to any tools available for use.

Anastasia Anisimova: I wanted to add a brief note to what was written above. I came across a phrase in Ksenia Evgenievna's book *"Karma, or the Law of Cause and Effect"*: "…a person who transitions from the warrior level to the ruler level must, as an 'entry ticket,' not only refine their own personal experience but also their ancestral experience. This is written in the informational conditions of the caste: only those with a long ancestral memory have the right to belong to the higher nobility. Those who transition from the warrior-ruler level to the mage level must also present their reincarnational experience."

I remembered Elizabeth I, who declared that she had "married England," and performed a ritual to embrace chastity. Well, whether it was chastity or not, I didn't exactly keep a candle for it, but she never actually married. She dedicated herself to the state.

Natalia: So, one of the tests for belonging to the highest caste is precisely the situation of being in a lower caste. Not to diminish yourself, not to try to pull them up, not to become arrogant, but to preserve your sense of self-worth in the most correct way, knowing who you are and who they are, while maintaining your own boundaries and respecting theirs.

Alexey Kobelev: If all warriors were born among warriors now, it would be very simple. It used to be that way. Now everything is mixed up, and these are the new rules of the game. You understand this correctly. Most warriors are born in the laborer castes, and less frequently in merchant castes. And the first goal is to get out of this "swamp," but unfortunately, this is where most people fail.

sveeik: Yes, about the swamp, you're absolutely right, that's exactly how it feels. But from my experience, I've noticed that after getting out of one swamp into a more dynamic and interesting environment, after some time you realize that this environment becomes a swamp too, and you want to get out of it just as much. Probably, it's an endless process...

Guest: Please tell me, I was taught that after the warrior's path comes the path of the monk (or, alternatively, the adept, the follower…). In general, from the same source, this is also a kind of warrior's path, with the difference that the monk is a step above and the monk can always take off the robe and pick up the weapon if necessary, and that their essence is the same, since the warrior fights external manifestations of lawlessness, while the monk deals with their internal "obstacles." And from the same source, only after completing the path of the monk can one transition to the level of a mage or ruler. In this caste hierarchy system, is the path of the monk (this function) developed within the warrior caste? And does this mean that an adept (monk, follower…) can only be someone who belongs to the warrior caste? And how should a person who was born with the feeling of being a monk find themselves—can they search for themselves in the warrior caste?

For example, I have a son, and in his early childhood, he could only imagine himself as a hero, and whenever asked his name, he would present himself as a hero by name and patronymic. At the same time, he doesn't like any kind of sports fighting, he's resilient but not inclined to physical exertion, so in the simple understanding of a warrior, he doesn't fit that role at all. However, he is deeply interested in religious teachings, as much as he can understand them at his age.

Yllymakh: From personal considerations, without claiming to speak the truth:

1. As I understand it, in Castaneda's system of castes, a monk is essentially a mage. A monk, or a mage, is someone who has understood (or strives to understand) the magical essence of the world, and now they are no longer interested in the social phenomena of the world. They seek their own connection to the Force, to study the world with its help and thus raise their level of development to that of their progenitor—to the level of the consciousness of God.

The struggle with internal obstacles is the tuning of the frequency of the channel, a spiritual path. This takes place at the first stage in the mage's caste, when the assemblage point is in the Heart Chakra—this is the level of extrasensory perception. When their own Force is found (status as a follower), the obstacles are removed and the channel is fine-tuned—the "gift" is revealed.

A warrior has a choice: either to become a mage or a ruler. But the path to becoming a ruler—crystallizing knowledge/skills for managing society—is the pinnacle of a warrior's path, and not every soul chooses it. Because it's like getting stuck at the warrior caste level, staying in the same grade for the second year. You will eventually return to the path of magic, but the soul's learning process will be prolonged.

A mage does not seek to govern society. The mage, at the warrior caste, has already gained the right to power, and now it is enough for them to control the ruler in order to control society as a whole. The goal of the mage is not governance, but to channel the will of their Force into our world.

2. A follower (of a channel, a deity) can be someone from the mage caste. A warrior refines their knowledge of society and their survival skills in it, but unlike merchants, they think not only of themselves—they care for others. And this care gives them the right to power. When a warrior discovers the Force and becomes its follower, they transition to another caste and become a mage.

A mage does not have the task of participating in social life—they have already learned everything about it while being a warrior. Some even as rulers. Therefore, the mage caste is outside of society. Inside the mage caste, there is a separate society (though the term is hardly suitable for a community of mages, as it is not a society, but rather a community, a caste). And there are their own gradations. At the first stage of tuning the channel, a mage is usually still connected to society by weak threads, but their number steadily decreases, because for the mage, society is only a testing ground and a place to channel their Force into the world. Extrasensory, Healer, Alchemist, Demiurge—these are already castes for mages. They are outside of society and focused on working with the channel.

3. I believe that if your knowledge of the human world is complete, and you have already acquired the right to power that the warrior caste grants, developed your skills in governance and functioning within the system, and have built a core of spirit and principles within yourself—your work in the mage caste is finished, and there is simply no need for you here. You are already in search of your own channel, that is, your spiritual path. However, if this is not the case—the inner core has not been developed, the right to power is still in question, and there are no skills for functioning within a hierarchy or system—then it's not yet time to rush into becoming a mage.

As Ksenia Evgenievna says, it is better not to pretend to be something you are not, so you don't end up making a lot of mistakes and having to return to your starting position, restarting the work while simultaneously digging through your own mess. The path from merchants to mages is much shorter than from imagined warriors to mages, then back to merchants, then to warriors, and again to mages. The key is to honestly assess yourself and your position, based on reality. Markers can be the rights given to you from birth and those you have acquired on your own, the system of fundamental principles, and the guidance of oracles—Tarot, runes, and the guidance of those who see/know. The system Ksenia Evgenievna teaches is beneficial because you must reach everything on your own, and such self-discovered knowledge is the most valuable. It's a bit difficult, but patience and effort, as they say...

If I've made any mistakes, I hope the esteemed teachers will correct me.

Guest: Thank you. By logic, the paths of the warrior and the monk are convenient to walk together. There is much in common regarding their relationship to property, settledness, goal-setting, the development of loyalty, and adherence to laws... A monk, however, is not yet a Master; he is simply an initiate in training. Perhaps there is a slight difference in their relationship to society, as the warrior is already not quite part of society. And after all, the king (monarch, emperor) possesses knowledge of magical laws at their foundation, they are taught this at some stage, yet they do not become a mage. On what path do they learn this then, if not the warrior's path? There is no separate caste of monks, after all.

Thank you for engaging with my question. Everything is clear now. From warrior—monk to the next level, emperor—priest— mage, they most likely transition through existential volume (which strengthens the right to power), depending on the "circles" in which this existential volume accumulates.

Yllymakh: According to Castaneda, there are only three social castes: laborers, merchants, and warriors. When a warrior first sees magic in action, they are intrigued, but they will never place their social interests below the interests of magic and God. Magic for them is merely a tool to solve their social tasks, but never the goal. This is why I categorized the monk as a mage. I think it's a kind of transitional stage from a warrior to a mage, with the Heart Chakra (Anahata) as the point of assembly.

At this stage, social interests become secondary—this is a remnant of the warrior caste on the path to becoming a mage. For the warrior, however, social interests are primary. That's the main difference.

Regarding the openness of today's castes, Ksenia Evgenievna has a video where she explains why, in the last two hundred years, since the beginning of the Age of Aquarius, castes have started to open up and intermingle. That is, a laborer can easily be born into a warrior kin, and a mage into a laborer family. The motto of Aquarius is "freedom, equality, fraternity," and this is realized in practice by dismantling the ancestral egregor. This is why there is confusion with the castes. Egregors want to guide all people to the principle: "Every life is born with zero rights, but with a wealth of knowledge, and each time I go through the entire path from laborer to mage in one life." This benefits all egregors but is not advantageous for people or their families.

As for determining one's caste, I suggest simply using facts. For example: A family has lived in the city for a long time. They left the village six generations ago—this is an indirect sign that about six generations ago, there was a transition from laborers to merchants. Merchants leave the village when they realize that everything in the world—goods, labor, objects, homeland, talents, even their own body—does not belong to them. From this point onward, their connection to the land weakens significantly, while their connection to society strengthens.

This kind of separation occurred in most Russian families during the Soviet years when the village was largely abandoned, families moved to cities, traded their sickle for a hammer, their gardens for stores, ancestral knowledge for school learning, traditions for money. The process began much earlier, and it continues today, with the peak occurring during the post-war Soviet years. Dachas, as a tribute to the transition from land to society, will eventually fade into the past.

Most of the relatives are connected to the system—this is an indirect sign that the family belongs to the warrior caste. They couldn't be forced to abandon their work in the system for money, status, or fashion during the turbulent 90s—in fact, especially not during those years. Stubborn, principled, they are often called "people with a backbone," "pillars," "everything rests on them, without them, everything will collapse." They don't swear, not because of circumstances, but because there is no such program in their subconscious. There are no circumstances that could morally break them. They know their business and will do it.

Most of the relatives are somehow connected to magic—witches, sorcerers, monks, priests, mysterious sectarians. To outsiders, they seem like a crazy family. No one tries to befriend them or get close. First, it's simply scary, and second, they don't particularly connect with anyone. Each lives in their own world, with their own interests, and years or decades may pass without seeing each other.

These are just my thoughts. If we discard the lyricism and simply look at the facts we have. If I was pushed out of the warrior caste, which I have plenty of indicators for, into the merchant caste, then I must have missed something in the merchant caste—I didn't notice provocations and quickly fell from being a mage into the merchant caste. But unlike real merchants, who don't know the way up and learn everything through trial and error, I should know how to go there the short way without meandering, since I've already been through this path. Well, I stumbled, forgot the rules, didn't notice the provocations, and tumbled into the merchant caste—what can I do? I'll have to quickly climb back up the path to avoid ending my life as a merchant. Because in the next life, I'll have to start from the merchant caste again—what's the guarantee I'll remember the short path upward?

Vitaly: I'll add a little. It seems to me that the merchant caste is guided by the principle of "Want—don't want, like—don't like." The motivating and driving force for people in the merchant caste is the principle of "want," meaning sexual energy. If something gives them pleasure, the merchant says, "Yes, this is mine," but if it doesn't, they'll say, "I know what needs to be done, but I don't like it." So, to pass the level of the merchant caste, one must not only understand the structure of creating companies, the relationships with government bodies, learn how to handle money, and be able to negotiate, even securing favorable terms for themselves.

VladimirA: Why do you think so? Merchants clearly understand the concept of profit—if it's profitable, they will do even things they don't like... It's more likely that warriors will do things "for something"—at the very least, to enjoy it, in addition to responsibility, or influence on the world, or seeking trophies... But a merchant, in my opinion, will play first and foremost for "what will I get out of this," and for the sake of profit, they'll clean toilets, hang around the corner, or sell Chinese junk... Half of traders do things they don't like, but once they make a profit, they start to like it...

Vitaly: Let's not confuse things. If a person is guided by the idea of profit, that doesn't mean they belong to the merchant caste. The ability to earn money is not the sole indicator of belonging to the merchant caste. Laborers are very good at this too, and the people you see at markets, various traders, or people cleaning toilets for money, in the majority are laborers. It is precisely the laborers who will do what they don't like in order to earn. They'll do it with force, unwillingly, but they will do it.

A merchant always does only what they like, and what they like is interacting with people, exchanging information. As a result, by doing what they like, they accumulate money, connections, and friends. Because they want this, they enjoy the process of accumulation, of creating something new (it's a game for them). They love the game (not the tedious and dull earning of money while standing at a market or cleaning toilets, even for a lot of money).

Merchants are those who create various business schemes, new companies, but they do it precisely because they enjoy it, because they want to—"playfully" acquiring new partners and friends. They "love" acquiring more sexual partners and simply making more money and acquiring things. Besides the accumulation process, merchants "adore" creating something new; it's business, or more precisely, business schemes, and naturally, expanding their circle of influence (new friends, new communications). Look at them—they are the ones who can and love to turn the unsuccessful into successful, the bad into good.

And a representative of the warrior caste is distinguished by responsibility and the level of duty. And warriors, in contrast, will not live by the principle of "want—I do, and want—I don't do," but will be guided by the principle of "need." That is, if it is necessary, they will go and achieve results. They win, they reach heights, these people are warriors in life.

raido9: *Reflections on Castes, or Why Laborers Don't Need Philosophy.*

The scope of the laborer's consciousness is limited to the life-death cycle, and it only looks beyond that within the framework of procreation. All attention is focused on the rhythms of nature; time is slow, consumed by labor and work. The tradition that such consciousness is part of answers all emerging questions and is seen as the ultimate truth. Tradition can take many forms: it can be religion, or it can be the television. Tradition dictates what to love, what to hate, what is good, and what is evil. For a person steeped in tradition, everything is simple and clear. This consciousness does not doubt, it believes—there is no need to philosophize, for everything is already known, and abstract reasoning, which cannot be touched or felt, does not provide nourishment.

The merchant will consider tradition from the perspective of profit. They will choose the tradition that brings them success, exalt it, and remain within it as long as it is beneficial. However, if the tradition leads to failure, their consciousness will either break, acknowledging defeat, or it will change the tradition. It will be difficult, but the motivation of profit and results will enable them to take that step. Their sense of good and evil stems from what is profitable, and the tradition may be changed. Profit, in the broadest sense of the word.

A warrior's consciousness is significantly different. They are curious, constantly learning and exploring, including philosophical views and different perspectives on values, interacting with various traditions. The warrior will seek their own path and remain loyal to it until the end, even if it is not profitable, not fashionable, or even if it brings death—there are examples of people who sacrificed their lives for an idea. The scope of such consciousness goes beyond life and death; it sees further than their own life. The most important thing for a warrior is the idea they serve—its growth, development, preservation, and continuity. Their consciousness is close to the second circle of fundamental principles, akin to priesthood.

Rulers are few. I recently heard an opinion that monarchy is the most just form of governance, as the ruler is chosen by God, in the sense that they are prepared from birth to be a ruler. In our time, becoming a ruler and developing one's consciousness to this level is no simple task...

The most interesting thing is that, no matter how much progress occurs, including technological progress, such as now with the availability of knowledge (the Internet), the ratio of laborers, merchants, warriors, and rulers is roughly the same as it was in ancient times. In that case, can we truly talk about the evolution of human consciousness as a whole?

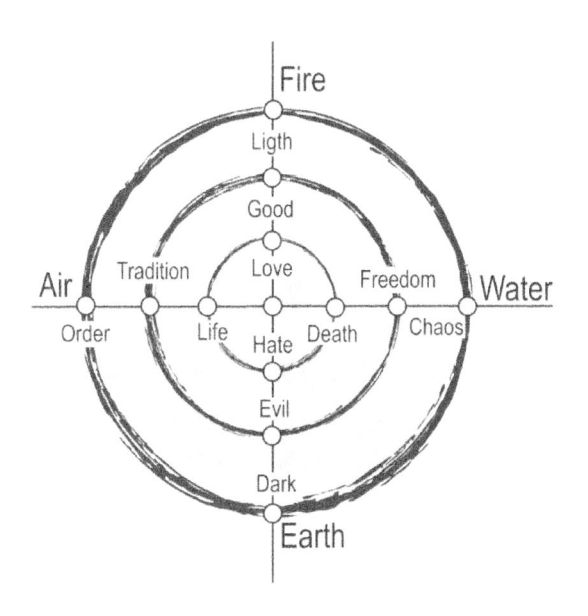

Three Magic Circles Scheme

Olga Chernova: Friends, I have a question. If a person has magical abilities from birth, can they belong to the castes of laborers, merchants, or warriors? Or do they belong to the caste of mages?

Biatana: It seems to me that a caste cannot be determined by just one parameter (trait)—the presence of abilities. We need to consider what rights the person has, how they realize those rights, and where their assemblage point is. In other words, everything must be taken into account as a whole.

Ekaterina NM: Reading how colleagues have discussed the theory of clothing in different castes, I wanted to refer to the past, a time when it was actually possible to determine a person's caste with greater certainty by their clothing. A time when the principle of blood still worked, when older and younger souls incarnated in the corresponding families.

Let's start with the nobility—let's say, they are the warrior caste. What did they wear? Corsets, heavy dresses embroidered with gold, silver thread, and gemstones. The weight of such a dress could easily rival that of armor. And how many discomforts did these lovely ladies endure to achieve a wasp waist by wearing corsets? And everyone wore them without exception, sometimes even breaking ribs to wear a corset, but they wore them. What about the men? Wigs, breeches... All of this corresponded to their status, but there was no talk of comfort.

Merchant caste. Clothing was previously regulated not only for the nobility but also for other layers of the population. Nobles wore one type of clothing, merchants wore another, and laborers wore a third. Please note, wearing clothes from another class was not just impossible due to cost; it was prohibited because it didn't correspond to a particular societal layer. Clothing was a business card and a display of "I belong to this society." If a merchant wore noble clothing, they could be punished for it. For example, there were specific colors in clothing that only the royal family could wear.

From this, we can see that the foundation of dressing in a particular manner was regulated, and there was a specific fashion in each era.

And the caste of laborers. Let's recall what a girl used to do in the past, one of her tasks? She would embroider and sew her dowry. If you visited museums, you might have seen laborer costumes. These were not silk outfits, but they were very beautiful and harmonious. Every sleeve, collar, hem, belt, apron, etc., was embroidered with protective embroidery, and each embroidery told a story about its owner. The dress had a sacred meaning; through the dress, you could see whether the girl was still a maiden or already a woman. It was a carefully thought-out costume, from the first thread to the last. And if any housewife in the village wore a soiled dressing gown, she would be branded as a dirty woman, and no one would marry her, etc.

In today's world, the principle of blood has been removed, and the layers of the population have mixed significantly. Fashion changes not every century, not every half-century, not every decade, but every year. Souls are born in more complex conditions—not in their own caste. The way people dress today is more related to personal preferences or their profession, not caste. Based on this, determining a caste by clothing is very presumptuous.

Radium: All people gather reserves, they collect something.

Laborers gather food—cheese, sausages, pickles, jams, grains, flour by the sack, potatoes, sugar, and they dry bread.

Merchants gather money—gold, diamonds, securities, assets, liabilities.

Warriors gather skills—abilities, victory algorithms. "How is this done? Can I do it? I'll go check."

For rulers, connections are important—friends, enemies, friends of enemies, enemies of friends, entourage, admirers, talent worshippers, electorate.

Therefore, for a laborer, it doesn't really matter what the work is, as long as they can come home afterward, where their best friends are... the television, the sofa, the fridge.

A merchant chooses where he will be paid more and pay less.

A warrior chooses the work that will teach him something new, open new horizons.

A ruler will be where they can become an important figure—where they can be feared and respected.

Wayfarer: Hello, Radium. Regarding rulers, I don't agree with you. It seems you're describing a modern merchant-ruler with puffed cheeks from pastries and vanity. The true ruler has a completely different mindset, understanding responsibility for their actions, seeing cause-and-effect relationships, and having a sense of time.

As an example of the mentality of a female ruler, I can recommend (off the top of my head) the movies *"Young Victoria"* and *"Grace of Monaco"*. Victoria was a woman born into the ruler caste, and Grace Kelly was a woman who entered this caste through marriage.

Radium: Hello, Wayfarer. What motivates this understanding, vision, and sense? What makes a person feel responsible and aware of time? What is the cause?

Wayfarer: Radium, this is determined by the position of the assemblage point. For a ruler, the assemblage point is on the buddhic level. The body of beliefs and values is active, and they themselves, one could say, are the embodiment of the idea. Grace Kelly managed to elevate her assemblage point to occupy a dignified place next to her husband in the eyes of her subjects, while Queen Victoria was prepared for the throne from childhood. And you are correct in saying that the proper selection of a team (entourage) is of immense importance.

At the Department of Elemental Magic, the particularities of worldviews held by representatives of different castes (not only this, of course) are experienced practically. It's better to feel it once on your own skin than to fantasize about it a hundred times, though contemplation does bear fruit.

Radium: From Grace Kelly's biography, we know that she was not recognized in her childhood; her brother and sister were the hope and pride of her parents. Grace became a model, then an actress—what was she searching for? When she married the prince, everything became like it was before, like in her childhood—she wasn't herself, she wasn't accepted fully by everyone.

When she asked the padre what would happen if she divorced, what did he answer? That it would mean she had failed. It would be a failure for her as the Princess of Monaco. And what did she do? She went to an etiquette teacher. She learned the language, history, manners, and the rules of hierarchy. What did the teacher tell her? That as a royal person, she is an object of intrigue. She learned this lesson too. What did she say at the ball? That she simply wanted to change the world for the better to the best of her ability.

Change the world? Why change it? When you can change the world, that means you are not a nobody, right? That you matter, that you influence something. You are an important figure. Of course, this doesn't sound as noble as "assemblage point on the buddhic level." But the location of the assemblage point has its reasons.

You say the ruler is the embodiment of an idea. Which idea?

Wayfarer: Radium, the motive for marriage? But is the motive really that important? The prince proposes, why not? Perhaps, the choice of Princess Grace Kelly by Prince Rainier III, not from the ranks of European princesses but from Hollywood stars, was a strategic move. I don't claim to be an expert on Grace Kelly's biography, but I think that in reality, things were a little different from how they were presented in the film. Let's say, in the film, the motive for her self-improvement was the desire to save her family and rekindle her husband's interest in her.

Yes, she studies etiquette—every society has its own rules of behavior, and one must master them. Language is not just a tribute to the people whose princess you are, but also a path to understanding their mentality, to understanding their cultural code. History, similarly, plus an understanding of cause-and-effect relationships in the context of international relations. She wanted to cancel the charity ball against the backdrop of an empty treasury—logically, from a rational perspective, but it conflicted with Tradition = a mistake.

The speech Kelly delivers at the ball—those "rosy roses." I don't know if she really gave this speech or if it was invented by the screenwriters. What matters is that she mastered one of the tools of the ruler caste— the right word, said at the right time (or the opposite), can influence the course of history. According to the film, she used the traditional charity ball as a chance to smooth over the increasingly tense conflict between Rainier and De Gaulle, and she succeeded.

In my opinion, equating the aspiration for power with possessing it is not entirely correct. In the first case, the assemblage point can be anywhere, but certainly not on the buddhic body. The reason is the same as in all other cases—it's about the level of consciousness development. To retain power, the assemblage point[17] must be on the buddhic plane. Nicholas II couldn't do it.

What idea's embodiment? Any idea. The one that the ruler's warriors serve, to which they voluntarily dedicate their time (and life). National identity, the Great October Revolution, or Nazi nationalism.

---

[17] The assemblage point on the buddhic body indicates that consciousness primarily operates with global meanings rather than simple concepts.

Fatamorgana: In this life, I had to take an exam in Vedic philosophy. Naturally, I had to study the varnas thoroughly—this is the traditional word for caste. Europeans started calling them castes, and the word "casting" has the same root and means selection. So, while studying the issue, I came to the following conclusions: belonging to a caste or varna is determined by the individual's goals and values. Nowhere in the Vedas does it say that caste is determined by birth and that you cannot change your caste during one lifetime. However, the ways of developing consciousness are given. I think that caste division by birth, without the right to transition, was invented for the purpose of control and subjugation. To keep people from sticking out. The harmful misconception about the impossibility of transition still sits in people's heads, even in fairly enlightened and European minds: maybe later, I will reincarnate into a higher caste, but for now, I'll suffer here, where I was born.

When I entered this School and began studying the materials on the caste system, I was once again convinced of how well I fit into my place. All these things, I understood by myself after long and painstaking thought. But here—there is a complete and very logical educational system, methods of transition, and monitoring during transformation times.

Bluefire: In one of the videos, the respected K.E. spoke about how the system of castes by birth was mixed by the leading religions, such as Christianity and Judaism. And if, in the past, someone born, like Buddha, in a royal family was not just marked by birth but came ready to rule, now, in a royal family, someone like... Charles, the Prince of Wales, can be born—royal by birth, but not ready to rule. Therefore, his mother waits for her grandson to mature, and she is already well over 90!

Fatamorgana: Yes, I also remember that video, where the caste system was mixed with both religions and revolutions. In our country, the warrior caste was destroyed with particular cynicism. And now warriors are born into the environment of other castes and must prove their right. Through fierce struggle—that's what makes them warriors.

Charles, most likely, does have the right by birth. But waiting for a smarter and stronger heir is a very reasonable decision. A strategic move, nothing personal.

Skog: Hello, colleagues. I'm excited to share a discovery. "By chance," I came across a video on YouTube. Here are some quotes on the topic:

"A merchant sees only the hierarchy of money. He doesn't see any other hierarchy. A warrior sees the social hierarchy ('epaulets') and understands how hierarchical systems are structured. A priest—he doesn't care about hierarchies, he sees the meaning. But for the priest, the merchant is important, because without the merchant, the priest will starve. For the merchant, money is the scale, everything can be measured by it, it is the only scale. As soon as you allow an alternative, you get different social hierarchies, which the merchant doesn't understand. He only has one question: if you're so smart, why aren't you rich? Merchants don't like families, because 'don't let your brother grow taller than you.'"

Remis: A very conditional picture. It's like a still frame from a movie. People are living beings, whose existence stretches across time. Despite all our primitiveness, we are subject to many changes. Development is a constant and endless process. Anyone who avoids development fades into non-existence.

Therefore, the quotes you provided are good for grasping the principle, but not so useful for applying them to people: linear thinking too eagerly seizes the opportunity to label and is too rigid when faced with the need to look at human change in dynamics—especially in long-term dynamics.

A merchant is not the same as another merchant, just as a warrior is not the same as another warrior, and a ruler is not the same as another ruler. Today one, tomorrow another, and in any direction.

Marina ts: I really want to analyze this with an example. A teenage girl. From a wealthy family, studying excellently, but at the same time, she constantly humiliates other children, sometimes hitting them in the face. She hits girls. When asked, "Why are you doing this?" she replies: "Because." Despite her parents' wealth, she periodically brings price tags from clothing to school. She wears bright makeup, dresses provocatively. I'm interested in your verdict. If needed, I can provide more details. I don't think she is being humiliated at home. The family is good, stable, and the parents are part of the parent committee.

Remis: Such behaviors often arise from several underlying causes:
- Formation of personal boundaries;
- Protection and reinforcement of personal boundaries;
- Testing others' boundaries for the possibility of expansion, with the aim of redistributing resources (any resources, regardless of goals or their absence);
- Establishing one's position in the social hierarchy, securing and defending status;
- Attracting attention, attempting to externalize an internal crisis in order to find a solution through external means;
- Realization of a "revenge" program, based on a whole range of possible reasons, etc.

As you can see, there are many triggers, and they almost never occur in isolation. They are much more likely to be encountered in combination, mutually conditioning and reinforcing each other.

It is also important to remember that when you say it is a prosperous family with good parents, you are making that judgment based on your (regardless of where it comes from) system of coordinates, and as a result, your own evaluations. In the mind of the teenager, this picture may be very different, even the opposite. Accordingly, they will see this same reality in a completely different way—not the way you see it. Multiply that by the hormonal storm, the many problems and challenges they have to cope with (and how to cope with them—who knows), and you'll understand that this could drive anyone to despair and to the wildest forms of behavior.

In this specific case, we might end up with, as one possibility (and I emphasize—just one of many possible options!), the following picture.

The adolescent environment is one of the most aggressive environments in general. Any difference, as long as you do not assert or defend your right to it and do not make it an advantage or exclusivity that grants authority, is seen as your weakness. And, rest assured, this weakness will be ruthlessly attacked—no matter how long it takes, until you are drowned.

The girl, as you say, is from a wealthy family. Perhaps not everyone in this group is in the same position, and teenage envy is quite an experience. I don't know about her appearance or her opinion of her own looks, but that's also an important factor. If her wealth has become a reason for mockery, trolling, and even bullying, it's clear that this is a problem for two reasons.

Firstly, because the girl understands that this wealth is not her achievement, and there will be a connection to "it's the parents' fault" within her. That is, on the one hand, she will understand that her parents are responsible for the situation, but on the other hand, she will enjoy the fact that she can afford what she wants, and this is not such a problem for her as it might be for many others. And here, she will feel gratitude.

To reconcile feelings of anger and gratitude within the framework of the same phenomenon and from the same source of that phenomenon is not an easy task for a teenager. It's something that not even all adults manage, by the way.

And that's just the first step. Let's go further.

If society does not accept you, you have the option to come to terms with it, give up, and start playing by its rules. In this case, it might mean risking ending up at the very bottom of the social ladder. That is hardly considered an acceptable scenario in this specific case. Therefore, it is necessary to find behaviors that will at least neutralize this scenario, and at most—create another, more advantageous one.

Here, the psyche finds the least resistance: to diminish the importance of the surrounding environment in your own eyes. For this to be possible, it needs to prove this thesis in reality. In the animal world, hierarchy is built on the principle of strength: whoever is stronger has power. In teenagers (not always, but often), the situation is generally not too different. Physical humiliation not only scares others, redistributes boundaries, and raises status, but it also gives a greater sense of self-confidence, legitimizes one's actions, and the whole scenario in one's own eyes.

And that's just the second step. But let's go further.

Price tags. And apparently, it's not about the smallest amounts. This is a continuation of the previous program. The motive is the same, just from the other side—the financial side. To put it simply, "you're beneath me because I can afford what you can't."

At the same time, it's a vicious circle, because the initial description about her being rejected by the group due to financial differences doesn't go away, and it only provokes new bouts of violence.

It doesn't stop there. Since, at this age, the issue of relationships with the opposite (or not-so-opposite) sex becomes paramount, she also needs to assert herself as a female. Hence, aggression toward other girls, i.e., direct competitors in the field.

And—note!—these are only fragmentary explanations. To deliver what you called a "verdict," more information is needed about this girl, her situation, her family and school relationships, her interests, friends, and sources of information. With such data, the picture could be fully outlined without assumptions. From what you described, it's possible to elaborate further, but it will still remain assumptions based on probabilities, and nothing more.

Marina ts: But I still don't understand her caste. She wants to dominate, and she's been like that since kindergarten. They separated her from one "rival" by putting them in different groups. She's a beautiful person, but she's annoying.

I have trouble with identification in general. A warrior? I really liked your response.

Remis: "A warrior?" Not necessarily. Competitiveness, in general, is inherent in all castes, but within each, it unfolds at its own level. If we reduce it to a universal principle, the first image that comes to mind is something like this:

- **Caste of Laborers**: Survive, live "no worse than others," and ideally, be "the top guy in the village." In this case, traditions, family bonds, and communalism are essential.
- **Caste of Merchants**: Multiply what you have, ideally infinitely. Here, the expansion of oneself beyond traditions, norms, and communalism is key. This is when we begin to see ourselves as independent and self-valuable individuals. Family—nearby. Friends—nearby. But the goal is to maximize yourself by projecting your ego outward. Money is the universal measure of such projection.

- **Caste of Warriors**: Belonging to something greater than yourself, serving an idea (which one is individual) as a principle of existence, striving for the realization of an ideal/idea/norm, etc.
- **Caste of Rulers**: Managing large systems, maintaining security, ensuring controlled adaptability and healthy functioning of these systems at various levels.

In this case with the girl, it's likely to suspect the merchant caste. Though, of course, I could be wrong. As I said, there is little initial information.

Suhnny: In a magical sense, the level of wealth has nothing to do with castes. Castes define one's attitude and interests toward the world and others. If they are only interested in the material and at the same time despise everyone else, this is the lowest degree of the first caste. In Slavic terminology, they would be called *smerdy* (peasantry).

Phenix: Good day, everyone! Yesterday, I witnessed a vivid example of a merchant trying to nullify a warrior. And the fury when it didn't work. The first truly believes the second is a fool for refusing to sell their time and knowledge for money. (As I understand it, he's irritated that he couldn't take the warrior's power.) As one mage said, "What is normal for the first caste, is a pig for the fourth!" (An example from other castes, but the essence is the same).

I was deeply inspired by this warrior's act. Such pride in the caste. A tremendous impulse. I came up with an analogy... in professional sports, at the level of Candidate Master, all merchants leave the sport. Only warriors remain. Because above, the goals of daily struggle with oneself and battles, the thirst for competition, and rivalry drive them. Titles, awards, are just background; the goal becomes secondary. And on a subtle subconscious level, I noticed (I'm at the level of transition, so I don't want to offend anyone) that, despite all the attributes of merchants, their confidence, power... there is an aura of fear. Not in the direct sense, but in some magical sense... And this is very noticeable. On the other hand, you can immediately recognize a warrior, regardless of their social status. A warrior radiates an aura of Power, and this cannot be confused with anything. High-level merchants try to imitate this power, but it cannot be faked. It must be earned. Therefore, when a true warrior interacts with a merchant, regardless of material status, the latter always subtly tests the warrior's "worthiness," trying to suppress them... If they can't, they immediately "know their place." As I understand it, all of this operates at the energy level. Subconsciously.

Remis: A thesis-based discussion about merchants and warriors.

We know that people are divided into castes. There are four castes: laborers, merchants, warriors, and rulers. Today, I would like to reflect on the parallels and differences between two of them: merchants and warriors.

Let's start with warriors. A warrior is an independent combat unit. And by stating this, we are dealing with two theses, each of which requires explanation. When we speak of the independence of a warrior, we imply their conscious need for freedom of self-determination. When we talk about a warrior as a combat unit, we imply their ability to be free, i.e., to defend their freedom and use it as a resource for personal development.

Here we can see certain parallels with the merchant caste. Representatives of the merchant caste must also, to a certain extent, separate themselves from the laborer caste, clearly detach their consciousness from the communal lifestyle of the laborers. For them, freedom is the ability to be free from the conditions and limitations of the previous caste (freedom from), and a certain degree of independence thus acquired is a necessary requirement for their development in the new role. In this way, freedom becomes the means of acquiring independence, and the focus shifts to themselves.

Since the merchant's attention is focused on themselves, a universal criterion must be introduced to evaluate results, to understand whose strategies are more successful and whose are less so. This universal criterion became money.

Warriors, separating themselves from merchants, also need to acquire freedom—an even greater freedom than merchants. However, a quantitatively greater freedom in this case cannot play a key role—it must be qualitatively different. That is why a warrior's freedom is not a merchant's freedom from, but a freedom for. This freedom is a conscious necessity, if you will—a duty or a price that must be paid for the opportunity of personal development.

If the merchant extraverts themselves into the world, engaging with universal systems of evaluation, then the warrior, on the contrary, introverts the world into themselves, rejects universality, and finds their own path, where the criteria for evaluation become subjective factors: their own assessment of themselves and their development within the realization of the idea—the meaning they have imposed upon themselves and for which they consider themselves responsible.

Thus, the key difference lies in the quality of the response to the question "Why?". The warrior sees this as their mission, the meaning of their activity always being greater than their own personality, and the results of their victories outlive them, independent of their will. The merchant gets involved in the competitive game, and in their eyes, it has intrinsic value— the point of this game is to play, and it is a self-contained and finished process that does not require additional motivational grounds.

This same difference forms the basis for motivation. For a warrior, because they are introverted, the concepts of nobility, honor, dignity, and duty become fundamentally necessary, as they are part of their self-identification, a kind of inner tuning fork. For the extraverted merchant, these concepts are not yet obligatory, because they are not part of the set of qualities needed for the merchant's game. Simply put, they do not convert into quick money, and therefore, they are meaningless. Since the warrior starts to operate over longer periods, they can no longer afford short-sightedness—the reality does not tolerate such irresponsibility.

Typically, the typological motivation is different: where merchants tend to prefer status and wealth as motivators, warriors are more likely to prefer self-sufficiency and uniqueness.

If the merchant caste develops algorithms for social connectivity (useful me + useful others) and converts it into money, then the warrior caste develops algorithms for individual connectivity (different parts of me, which I develop and bring together into a harmonious whole) and converts it into realized meanings.

Thus, where the merchant sees the monetary game as their finished ontological meaning, the warrior goes even further and understands that this game is only one of the tools necessary for the development of consciousness and personality, a kind of developmental stage, behind which lie deeper and more important things in terms of meaning and content. And it is these things that become the object of their inquiries and aspirations. In other words, money goes from being a meaning to a tool, and the process of acquiring money changes from a meaningful pursuit to an instrumental one. And this tool becomes a means to realize the meanings that the specific warrior considers important. At this point, the warrior no longer has the foresight to understand that any such meanings are just tools for maintaining and realizing a whole complex of systemic factors, each of which plays a role in establishing, maintaining, and spreading a certain ontological order in space-time, without which all previous ontological levels, in general, will lose their meaning. A warrior who truly understands and accepts this becomes capable of moving to the next level—the caste of rulers, where they will work on developing algorithms for forming, maintaining, and spreading such orders and the complex systemic factors that support them.

If a ruler begins to lead a nation directly under the guidance of a divine ruler and does so more effectively than merchants do under the guidance of egregores, then questions arise about their necessity as such. Everyone wants to live.

It's easier, if possible, to prevent people from going anywhere, forever provoking, distracting, and tempting. They manage quite well themselves.

On the topic of a temporary pause in self-development.

Menshikova: A person can generally allow themselves anything they want. No one is watching them 24 hours a day. There is only internal control, and it works differently for each caste. A laborer will say, "What's the big deal?" A merchant will try to find an explanation and justification. A warrior will consciously retreat from the rule—not justifying themselves but consciously going for a loss now to be able to do what they cannot do today, tomorrow.

Rest is needed by everyone. Both those who are on the path and those who have already achieved something must reckon with the imperfection of their biology. If there is no need to harm oneself with heavy medications, it's better to retreat in those hours when retreat is necessary by definition. But a warrior, possibly a future mage, can turn their retreat into a ritual, give it meaning, introduce it into their routine and schedule. Then, an everyday action becomes a magical one, and the effect from it is multiplied many times. But this must be a conscious act, understanding what is happening right now and why; what effect is to be achieved in this situation, and what needs to be done tomorrow so that the time invested in the ritual of measured human existence will yield an effect that exceeds all expectations. A retreat before one battle may be a tactical step towards victory in another. But this must be seen and programmed before the process of laziness, not after, as merchants do. If it's after, it's pure self-deception.

VarvaraNjord: Hello, colleagues. Studying the runes of the Elder Futhark has greatly activated my thoughts about castes. I'd like to share here my reflections on the differences and transitions.

People from different castes have different needs. The realm of laborers is the realization of the need for security. There are shared traditions and maximum selfishness here. The desire for happiness through some material, everyday things. This is a narrow world of understandable, manifested space. What is the difference with merchants? Merchants expand outward, across connections worldwide, if they can. This is no longer a small, calm, and clear world, a safe one. It's a restless sea of people and quick decisions, with a hope for profit. Family and traditions can be tools for a merchant's expansion, or they may not be.

Therefore, their communication and interaction can happen outside the family to increase qualitative connections. And here, desires are shaken. They are the driving force. The merchant's need is good energy exchange with the world of people, and money is the measure of that.

In my personal experience, laborers have constant physical movement and suppression of those who act differently. As stated above, they don't eat with everyone and don't do things the same way. Plus, they must always do something physical. Well, indeed, their results and fruits depend on the amount of action. A person sitting and thinking, not acting for many days, is considered bad. This is evil to them. It's not like that for merchants. They understand that an idea can turn into money, that to solve problems, one needs time for reflection and learning.

How do I know this? My ex-husband and I met in the merchant caste. He was from the first levels, the first practices in the caste, while I was already at the later stages with accumulated experience. My family is made up of merchants. And this feature—always having to do something physically, not sitting still—was the most surprising for me. If a child reflects but sits still, they are considered lazy. Learning is just some burden that should be carried quietly and inconspicuously, preferably without standing out from the constant physical action of all the laborer-group members around. And as I saw, this very feature prevented them from transitioning to merchants.

They were always involved in small businesses, but it was always tied to the land, to physical work. Beekeeping, raising nutria, selling honey and fur. Everything is narrowly focused. No expansion. On their local level. I helped them expand to other cities and facilitated their transition into merchants. But there were still many steps to take for a shift in consciousness. My family is pure merchants. You can do nothing, the main thing is to learn, the main thing is to participate in the world, in its movement. Here, there were already limitations on thinking. If laborers simply don't give time and set external boundaries for development and reflection, then in the merchant caste, there is already an influence on thoughts. It's narrowing the circle of thoughts and ideas only within one's desires, fruitful connections, and the best possible deal with the world. No money? Start thinking positively, develop your wants, start communicating, and expand your circle of connections to the maximum, grab the best deals people can offer for joint affairs.

We didn't understand each other and still don't. Actually, I understand them now, but they don't understand me. I don't have those kinds of wants. I don't want to save up for a phone or work a year for a trip somewhere. My goal sometimes implied some trips, and then my mother would bloom with mutual understanding and unity with me. But it was short-lived. Because she waited, and still waits, for me to finally feel this craving for desire-building, this drive from multiple contacts, this good mood from the general field of interaction with people.

Further discussion is more difficult because I'm still completing the transition into the warrior caste. I endured in a merchant family environment. But oh, how difficult it was to detach my consciousness from my mother's imposed desires. Yet after gaining knowledge about the castes, everything fell into place, and my actions became clear. There was a tough period of "dying" in the merchant caste. Oh, how hard it was, I'll tell you. For a merchant, their own desires are the key to action. Without desires, there's death. For a merchant, connections with people are a means of growth and survival. Without these connections, they can't survive. I created conditions in my life for a transition. Loyalty to my profession, the absence of wants, constant relocations, and living with a clean slate. I worked in different cities, moved across the country, from apartments to houses. And now, looking back on this experience, I can say I was cleansing myself of merchant milestones in consciousness and strengthening myself as a warrior. Resilience and loyalty to the idea. How did my merchant environment perceive me? As someone heading towards death. And they tried to save me, pull me back into their mechanisms and consciousness.

I can't say I've completed the transition and passed it. Probably no, more than yes. But I already see this transition, understand it, and realize what's happening. What does it feel like? When part of my consciousness shouts: "There's death ahead, don't go, we sympathize with you and will help, just come back, or we'll lose you, you'll die a hungry death!" And another part of my consciousness says, "Look, you've been acting like a warrior for so many years, and everything is fine, there's Order in your life now, and there's always money." I just act like a warrior and through action, gradually convince my consciousness, showing it, like a little frightened child, that it's safe and normal here.

Meanwhile, money is my tool. Finally, I've started to have desires. Not the wants that drive me, but calm tasks that I fulfill within my Order.

In the warrior caste, Order is the highest bliss. After the sweet taste of fulfilling intense wants in the merchant caste, calm, stable, and deep Order is an absolutely wonderful experience, totally worth it!

Samorodok: Human life is short, and the attempt to live multiple lives in one is understandable. However, it rarely ends in success. There is a good saying: "Chase two hares and you will catch none." If a person has determined that they belong to a certain caste, they should act based on the "starting position" of that caste. To say that a mage needs to have their own business is, at the very least, foolish. When will they have time to practice magic if they are constantly forced to prove their "rightness" to merchants?

Using the algorithms of merchants and blindly copying their activities are two very different things. What a merchant applies to money, a warrior learns to apply to other things, for example, to knowledge. If a merchant sees an ineffective working algorithm in their own company and changes it to an effective one, why can't a warrior use the same algorithm, but for, say, ineffective knowledge at the moment?

The ability to isolate algorithms and apply them over a broader range allows one to bypass the "necessary" stage of becoming a warrior or a mage as a merchant. Moreover, in my view, the very act of trying to speak with merchants "in the language of money" is a provocation. Everyone should do their own work. There is nothing shameful for a warrior in seeking experience from a merchant or even a laborer, understanding that they possess experience and knowledge that the warrior lacks. But applying the acquired knowledge must come from an understanding of one's own caste affiliation. Each caste is self-sufficient. And each depends on the others.

Minevich: A warrior always answers for their actions: past, present, and future. The more knowledge, memory, experience, and skills one has, the deeper and more comprehensive the essence of what is happening becomes. In ancient Lithuania, there was a free-spirited estate—the nobility (the warrior caste). The term "shliach" (meaning "warrior" or "battle") originated from the words "clan" or "battle." This word was widespread in the Czech Republic, Poland, and modern Belarus. Within this estate, there was, of course, a hierarchical ladder, but it was unwritten. From a formal standpoint, there was no difference—this is the main phenomenon, a noble by definition was inviolable; no one had the right to encroach on their life or property. They were free to express their will and move around. Everyone had equally significant votes and the right to be elected. The nobility was strictly forbidden to engage in trade, usury, or craftsmanship under the threat of losing their status.

For this, they could be put to trial! The nobility protected their homeland on the battlefield—that was their duty. The worst thing was to shrink or become a usurer. The status was passed down through inheritance, or one could distinguish themselves with exceptional bravery on the battlefield. A person deprived of noble status would move to another estate—such as a merchant or servant caste.

The warrior's rank is high—to protect the idea. And one must be able to do this, constantly train, perfect their skill—these qualities are not acquired in a single moment—they are passed down through the kin or one must distinguish themselves on the battlefield!

prn.sn: How my path began. I was always looking for the answer to this question: which caste do I belong to? And after five years, the answer came. Perhaps this post will help someone. From personal experience, I want to note (but again, this is my personal experience) that everyone is unique, as some are potential warriors who move from the merchant caste to the warrior caste, some passed through the ruler's caste and returned to the warrior caste, and some have passed through everything, merged with the power, and came back to test themselves, cloaked in forgetfulness, beginning as warriors and recalling their divine purpose. So, I started at the beginning of the path, sat down, analyzed information about castes, was always drawn to mages, but also felt a certain connection with warriors. And then I stopped thinking about the caste system altogether and just kept moving forward. Over the course of five years, I kept walking. Falling, getting up, walking again, falling again, getting up. The main thing is to focus on developing consciousness, sacrificing all the parties, resting, and work, work, work! So, when a warrior establishes themselves in the caste, an absolute and clear understanding arises that you are a warrior, without doubt or fear. You haven't made this up, you know it! You've chosen the path. You understand all the hardships and limitations of the warrior's path, you realize that there is freedom of choice, but freedom isn't about being able to do everything you want, freedom is knowing that you can do anything you want, but you only do what you must. You clearly know and understand what you're doing, why you're doing it, and what will come of it. You know what you must do, and this duty is your conscious choice!

For a merchant and a laborer, duty sounds heavy and limiting, they seek the freedom to do whatever they can do, but for a warrior, duty is their path, their freedom, their strength. In the limits of duty, a warrior finds freedom and joy, unfolding as a warrior, strengthening their will, determination, and spirit. They do what they must do and feel joy for moving forward, breaking through obstacles, enriching themselves with experience, and strengthening their core. They have chosen the path, the duty, and the service. The warrior serves, and their service is in fulfilling their duty; this is how they maintain balance and harmony. The warrior has an idea. An idea that drives them forward, for which they throw themselves into battle every day with themselves, sharpening themselves like a blade. By moving forward for the idea, it is through this action that the warrior enriches, develops, and transforms themselves! Their highest idea is like a sunbeam that illuminates their path, their guiding star!

And they go! And when a warrior strengthens in their caste, they penetrate the idea much deeper! For all five years, the idea has guided me, but only recently did I realize its depth, width, and vastness. I realized why, for what purpose, and what to do with it, what the consequences will be from realizing it, why it's needed, and what is hidden behind the idea. And behind the idea, I realized the highest idea of my god, realized the power that, besides my own strength, leads and protects me, and I understood why this divine game exists.

The warrior knows what they are doing and why they need it!

The warrior sacrifices everything trivial, everything unnecessary, everything secondary for the idea!

Warrior despises fear! And consciously walks towards fear!

The warrior sees in volumes, perceives cause and effect! He looks to the root and sees deep.

The warrior has an unbending will!

Money for the warrior is only a resource, a flow from the warrior to the goal, but not the goal itself. It is a resource for embodying and realizing the idea. The warrior despises self-pity, does not pity others, for everyone makes their own choice and builds their own path, consciously or unconsciously, but it is still a choice.

And the warrior knows this!

The warrior is a true plowman. He controls his time and invests it in his own development and the achievement of his idea. The warrior despises lies, and the warrior either speaks the truth or remains silent. Only over time, as he ascends higher into magic, does the warrior become outwardly flexible, to avoid unnecessary questions, answers, suspicions, and so on. He begins to conceal his goals, ideas, motives, and himself, indeed, everything that the simple folk of Midgard do not understand.

The warrior has his own truth. A truth that he has examined, looked at from all angles, and is convinced that this truth is his, and always, under any circumstances, follows his truth. As long as you are a warrior, you will fight for your truth, but later you will realize that everyone has their own truth and that many do not need to know it. As you move up, the warrior becomes flexible, merging with everyone and everything (he already understands why and for what he needs this), begins to absorb other viewpoints and accept them, while remaining true to his own truth.

The warrior's rest is in his work. In his business, in his idea, rest is in honing and perfecting himself. The warrior rests when he works in his own development, his own idea. Other activities and entertainments, like those of merchants and laborers, are a waste of time for the warrior. In my case, the warrior completely and utterly detached himself from society, severed all ties, leaving only blood relatives, and immersed himself in self-knowledge and the expansion of his boundaries, knowing why and for what, faithfully following his idea. Only after years, as I began transitioning upwards, did the warrior start throwing himself into various social events, meetings, knowing why—to gain experience, to observe himself, and to hone himself, for the practice of magical tools. But again, the warrior in transition, the sorcerer, does not make a choice about where to go and where to be; his power guides him there for magical development and practice. Rest, in general, has a peculiar meaning for the warrior.

For a warrior who has settled in his caste, there will be no emotional swings. The warrior can control and regulate these. The warrior learns to control all of this and, later, will learn to consciously invoke certain emotions and feelings, and even suppress or regulate them. This becomes a tool for creation or destruction. The warrior is decisive, the warrior is conscious. He understands what he is doing and why, what he needs and what to do with it, and when his reality crumbles in the process of his self-transformation, there is no fear, only the desire to overcome himself, to perfect himself. The warrior is true to his word, for to the warrior, one who does not keep their word is worse than a wild beast. Thus, the warrior makes his word, his thoughts—heavy, in the sense of weighty, and as he transitions, his words and thoughts gain strength and meaning. The warrior is true. To himself, his power, his idea, his words, his ideals, his choice, his work.

And all the burdens of his path, which the warrior takes upon himself, his highest idea that he follows, those limitations that may seem incomprehensible to the two lower castes, are in favor of himself, and for the warrior, this is an honor. The warrior does not think about how difficult it is for him; the warrior thinks: "Yes, it is not easy! But only this way will I become stronger and harden myself, for every trial strengthens me and makes me better, better than I was yesterday. It is not easy! But it is a great honor for me to walk the path in the name of my idea, and a great honor to endure!"

The warrior always wins. For victory is a conditional concept, and the warrior knows this. Even if the warrior loses a battle, he knows: Space has shown him his vulnerability, his weaknesses, and here he must work on them. He will sit down, analyze what went wrong, see the cause and effect, recognize his mistakes, and take responsibility for everything that happened, extracting experience and drawing conclusions, becoming better than he was before the battle, for he has considered everything that was. This is how he has already won! He has won over himself. Yes, the warrior takes responsibility for himself and his life. And the warrior's mindset is: "The more difficult the trials, the more experience and understanding will be gained." The warrior does not seek to live a calm, even life. "Life is a journey, I'm on a drakkar, sailing towards the sacred star," and trials and hardships are only a joy, for he knows why.

And yes, the pendulum of time for him is quite wide. He looks far back and far ahead. How far, I cannot say, I think it is individual. I encompass my past lives, so each one will be different. But what is certain is that the warrior does not live in the "here and now," but is present in the here and now.

In our Homeland, they say: "What kind of character are you if you cannot lay the foundation for your destiny a thousand years ahead?" Draw your own conclusions.

In general, runes help! The great gift of the Great!

It is the runes that are the tool of the warrior's becoming, and after that, each will make their own choice about where they go.

Yulia Yuna: How does a warrior fit into the realities of modern life? What if a warrior is swept into freelancing? And what if there's a family? With children? For a long time, I really wanted to learn to trade. I took courses. I acquired the skills of a salesperson. And yet, I do sell! But, unfortunately, not products, but myself.

Every time I need to sell, it's not the product that's bought, but me and the interaction with me, as a "trustworthy person."

And now, here's a life hack. Because it has been painfully learned over months.

Selling is difficult not because I have to take money for a service, but because I need to explain that everything will be done honestly and on time—which, for me, is self-evident, and it's even written in the contract.

There's offline work and online work. I started noticing a pattern: the more I help for free in one area, the easier it is for "money to come" in another. Right now, I'm dynamically switching: one moment I realize something in one area, then I make financial updates in another, then I switch again—and it goes in a circle. So, here's the question. Does the fact that I've found such a mechanism mean that, in reality, I am a merchant at heart and should stop pretending to be a warrior?

Suhnny: Familiar situation... You help, help the merchants, and they think it's just how things are... No, dear ones, debts will have to be repaid.

It simply means you're not doing what you're meant to be doing.

Any warrior would have no problem solving a merchant's problems, since this experience has already been traversed in an existential sense. The real question is that the whole of modern civilization is built on merchant principles, and there's practically no place for warriors in it (hence, one has to find ways to apply their abilities).

Mira: I've noticed that all warriors are very self-contained. They are quieter, they know how to listen. It's very hard to influence them. If they've decided something, their position cannot be changed. They will only do what they've decided. They won't deviate from their path. They don't fall for any manipulation. You could say, they are a complex caste. Or "dark horses." Some brain manipulations and decisions. They're not like merchants. Merchants are "simpler horses." That's why they can suffer greater monetary losses. Any merchant loses money and often falls for fraudsters. Warriors are quite different. They are less impulsive, more thoughtful, balanced, and calculating. They produce results that cannot be easily altered. The warrior caste is purer. Merchants can't stand warriors. I've noticed that when it comes to castes, a merchant is all emotions, while the warrior is calm. Maybe not all are like this, but that's my experience. A merchant's theme is, so to speak, how to turn 100 units into 1,000. They care only about money. Nothing else interests them.

Not all warriors have their own homes. But their level is still higher in everything.

Klevtsova Daria: In my opinion, a warrior can only not have a home for one reason—his own choice/belief. But if a warrior experiences discomfort in life due to not having his own home, that's a minus for him. He is hierarchically above, and thus must possess the skills of the lower castes. Figuratively speaking: if you have nothing to eat, go earn and buy—merchant methods. If you can't earn, go plant potatoes, grow them, and harvest them—methods of the laborers. A warrior must be capable of all of this. But if the warrior really has to go plant potatoes, it's worth thinking carefully about that...

Natalia A: When you don't know who you'll have to fight tomorrow—that's not a warrior, that's a laborer, cannon fodder. Just like a priest or mage who doesn't know where God will send them—that's not a priest or mage, it's the same laborer who relies on divine will.

The higher the caste, the broader the amplitude between past and future, the more information your consciousness can process. This consciousness sees cause-and-effect relationships in volumes. It understands that what it does today will lead to a certain chain of events, which will unfold over a period of time. What was done a year ago will give these results today, three years from now, these results, and ten years from now, others. The longer your memory, the further ahead you can plan, your actions are not discrete; they are extended.

Klevtsova Daria: Friends, here are some thoughts. In discussions about caste interactions, particularly concerning merchants, there seems to be a certain dismissive attitude. I see this as not entirely accurate, at least according to the fundamental magical law: "there is no thing better than another thing." All professions are necessary, all professions are important. I think there's a bit of a mix-up between concepts: there are merchants—and then there are traders. If a merchant starts falling in consciousness, openly degenerating, they become a trader. And that's a pity.

But a true merchant will continue to grow and develop. Often, this development is horizontal, but by establishing a foundation of material and financial security, the merchant opens up the possibility of moving their consciousness upward. There's a saying among the Chinese: "If a Chinese person hasn't tricked someone by the end of the day, they feel like they've wasted the day." Look at China's economy...

"You can't build a business on deception." Oh, but you absolutely can. What percentage of truth is shown in advertising? And how much manipulation of consumer consciousness is involved? Lying is not prohibited in this world. It would be too easy to live in a world where you know you're never lied to and always get information that perfectly reflects reality. Therefore, for progress, for moving forward, we must learn: first—to identify lies, and second—to turn them to our advantage. In other words, gain a benefit for ourselves.

"Read Ostrovsky, see what the merchant's word meant. Deals were made simply on words." That's true, and it appears in much older sources as well. In the *Primary Chronicle*, it's mentioned that merchants used to seal agreements with oaths to Veles and Perun. But we must not forget that warriors are not forbidden from doing merchant business, either a thousand years ago or today.

If a merchant loses something to a laborer simply through physical superiority, it indicates that the merchant neglected the methods of the lower castes—safety and preservation. Previously, physical and material protection prevailed, and now legal protection is also important.

For example, it's necessary to hire and fire employees correctly on paper so that they don't begin to threaten with labor inspections and taxes, demanding money from the employer. There are known cases like this.

Daria: I'm reading the thread and decided to share my observations. I live in Africa, on an island. Among the islanders, laborers dominate, but the merchant caste seems to be the most prominent. Everyone has their own business, but about a third of them don't keep their word. They evaluate you only based on your financial capacity. I notice it, it's unpleasant, but curious.

For them, money is a religion. In no other country have I witnessed such a reaction to finances. Just mentioning "money" in conversation makes a person rip apart, either from:

a) aggression,

b) envy.

When I say "rip apart," I mean it literally. Their body starts shaking chaotically, and their eyes fill with blood. I've tried many times to have dialogues with different people here, and the reaction is the same.

Collective consciousness.

The most interesting part is that I began observing myself. I've always had an easy relationship with money—if it comes, it goes, then it will come again. But suddenly, and I'm not sure why, I wasn't spending at all, and my savings disappeared. Now there's this permanent state of "enough for needs." Even when everything runs out, a source for the "living wage" appears again. I had never noticed this before in my life. Now, it's enough only for the essentials and a cup of coffee. What is this?

Ekaterina NM: Mini-essay. Quotes and actions from the anime *Spice and Wolf*.

The story unfolds in the first four episodes, and I will describe what pertains to this topic. There is much more in the later episodes, so anyone interested can watch it and find something for themselves. The main characters: Holo the Wise Wolf—she is the goddess of harvest who has lived a long time in one of the villages. Lawrence—an itinerant merchant, the main protagonist (MP).

I will immediately point out that from the very beginning, if interpreted through the system, the main character met his god. From this moment, his life undergoes radical changes, and translating this into the language of the School, his *BM* growth accelerates. Many provocations occur in the protagonist's life thanks to the goddess, and each provocation leads to a series of consequences, lessons, and some personal benefit.

Significant situation 1:

When Holo the Wise Wolf and Lawrence make a deal and set off on their journey, they encounter a merchant along the way. They strike a certain deal with him. Their path leads to another city. Holo and Lawrence are riding in a cart, while the other merchant is walking on foot. Holo asks why he hasn't traveled with them. The MP answers her that he'll get there faster on foot, as the roads are muddy and traveling by cart would be much slower. At this point, the Wolf laments that merchants are always in a rush, never seeing what's happening around them. To which the MP responds: "TIME IS MONEY, a minute can be turned into a coin." This, perhaps, is one of the key components of a merchant's mindset. At this moment, the Wolf laughs, and Lawrence tries to explain to her that laborers also value time, spend it carefully, and notice its passing. Holo's response: "Laborers don't think about time—they only know WHEN it's time. Dawn—time to rise, before noon—time to plow, after lunch—time to mow the grass. In spring, they rejoice in the bloom, in summer they revel in the greenery, in autumn they celebrate the harvest, and in winter they long for spring. They don't notice the passage of time."

Notice how accurately the difference in the perception of time between the laborer and the merchant is highlighted. The merchant is in a hurry, racing somewhere, trying to earn more, thinking about the future, planning for a longer period of time. The laborers live by the seasons, they don't think about the future—it's unnecessary for them. The merchant considers what he can sell for years ahead, while the laborer cannot grasp such a timeframe because he is dependent on the "whims" of nature. Different levels of possibility.

Significant situation 2:

Holo and Lawrence are traveling to another city. The MP asks the goddess: "How many centuries will I need to gather experience to understand all of this?" The goddess laughs and says that he is very perceptive. Here it is shown that if the MP were to go on the path alone, it would take him a long time, possibly many lifetimes, to gain such experience. However, under the guidance of his god, this path can be traversed much faster.

Significant situation 3:

The MP is transporting animal pelts for sale. He strikes a good deal with the buyer. Before this moment, Holo the Wise Wolf piles a mountain of apples on the pelts. (If anyone watches the anime, pay attention—had the MP handled the apple purchase differently, the outcome would have been different. This was a sort of test by the goddess.) As a result, the fur absorbs the scent of apples. The Wolf is sly and tells the buyer that these are special pelts that smell of apples. The other merchant, believing her, buys the pelts at two or three times the original price. And here's the quote that partly represents the merchant's principle: Holo to the MP: "I would not call it a lie, but a valuable lesson for a reasonable price. To be angry or upset in this situation is foolish. An adult person always appreciates cunning for what it is." This is roughly how merchants operate. The deal was supposedly honest, but the merchant will never pass up an opportunity for profit. A merchant's honor has nothing to do with a warrior's honor, and that's why the word "honor" is not quite appropriate when talking about the merchant caste. A merchant wouldn't be a merchant if he didn't try to outsmart his opponent. And for a merchant, everyone they interact with is a competitor for profit. This phrase "a thief is not a thief until caught" is exactly applicable to the merchant caste.

Fatamorgana: While analyzing the caste system, I noticed one thing. It's no secret that our country is ruled by merchants. Probably the same goes for other countries too. They write laws for merchants in a language understandable to merchants. And they protect their caste. This is why many people struggle to start their own businesses. A laborer doesn't have the qualities, the "existential volume," to register a business, handle taxation systems, report correctly and on time, or take advantage of subsidies. They either stay in the shadows and can't make a decent income, or they have to pay real merchants for consultations, support, etc. Only a true merchant, with the appropriate rights, can understand all the nuances of business in Russia. As a result, merchants have no competitors, laborers have no desire to develop or even engage in business, and warriors don't care about it at all.

Ekaterina NM: Belonging to a particular caste is not just a social status, but more importantly, the maturity of "I Am". Each caste has specific tasks to be accomplished.

Money is just an external manifestation, a criterion reflecting something, but it is not a complete indicator. Transitioning from one caste to another is determined by internal growth.

In each caste, a person works through their tasks. The merchant caste is driven by the value of: striving for pleasure and profit. Profit is not only in monetary terms but in a broader sense. For merchants, the satisfaction of their own desires is the primary goal. Their motivation is to earn more money in order to fulfill their desires, build more connections to become more significant, and have the ability to realize their desires.

Merchants possess qualities like cunning and agility. These people have many ideas, which, when realized, bring them money. Merchants like to be at the center of attention, bask in luxury, show off their significance, demonstrate some arrogance towards the laborer caste, and want to assert power over them. They delegate the "dirty" work to laborers and indulge in their importance. Merchants are often vulgar, trying to show off their lavish lifestyle, with no sense of moderation. If a golden chain is needed, it must be the thickest. They are not concerned with aesthetic beauty; the main motivation is to display their wealth. Family is valuable to a merchant, but it is seen as a reflection of their own feelings, with importance placed on experiencing attachments, again for the sake of pleasure. Therefore, merchants often compromise their family duties, for example, by taking a lover to obtain new pleasures.

A person in the warrior caste has the potential for discipline. This drive aims to bring order both within themselves and in the external world. The motivation here is not to showcase significance, as with merchants, but the desire for order. The goal is to acquire knowledge and pass it on to others. The driving force is the aspiration for personal development. Money, connections, others' opinions, and SSI[18] take a back seat to the main goal, the idea the warrior lives for. Warriors are characterized by qualities such as a sense of duty, the value and weight of words, internal strength, and willpower. A warrior has a clear understanding of the caste system, but not due to a desire to fulfill personal pleasures, as with the merchant, but because of the natural ability to either lead or submit (to the ruler). The central focus is on a higher purpose. A warrior values their family, but their mission/idea remains their primary focus, and they are willing to sacrifice much for that idea, while still adhering to their sense of duty.

The transition from one caste to another signifies a full transformation of a person's values. A complete rewrite of their program and life priorities. It is precisely the complexity of replacing one set of values with another that explains why people often spend most of their lives in one particular caste, or even multiple lifetimes, due to an inability to learn a particular lesson.

You can determine which caste you belong to right now by the motives that drive you. It is crucial to answer honestly to yourself what values are most important to you. You can also look at your surroundings and notice which people you are oriented towards. From which caste do they come? Who do you consider your own? By answering these and other

---

[18] SSI — Sense of Self-Importance.

questions, you will find your answers and grow. Good luck.

Anastasia Anisimova: I wanted to add something from personal experience. I had the fortune of working at one of the most influential investment banks in the world. I can confirm that merchants at this level can possess causal AP (assemblage point) — not often, but they can. They clearly track cause-and-effect relationships, are incredibly smart, and often have academic backgrounds with a deep understanding of fields outside of finance, such as chemistry, biology, and physics — they invest specifically in these fields. Within the caste, there are different levels — lower ones (merchants who squander their savings due to weak will, lack of experience, and knowledge) and higher ones — merchants who invest in the development of science. The one thing that unites them is the drive for profit. The current of money is a powerful force that largely governs the world.

Klevtsova Darya: Here's another observation, colleagues. How do merchants solve everyday human problems of varying importance? A merchant will do everything possible to buy his way out of a problem. If a child is sick, they'll hire the best doctor, no questions asked! Sitting at home with a sick child for a week? Who's going to earn money? If it's a potential warrior currently passing through the merchant caste, they'll be more critical when it comes to problem-solving. They might even, unconsciously, categorize problems — distinguishing between things that can be solved with money and where more substantial resources like personal time and energy are needed.

From this observation, I've derived a principle: if a problem can be solved with money, it's not a problem — it's an expense. The key is to properly define the category of the problem!

Fatamorgana: I've also thought about this. Let's say a rich kid runs over a child. The rich kid's father comes to the child's father and says, "I'll pay for the best doctors, rehab in Switzerland, I'll throw in whatever you ask. And legally, you won't win anything; I have everything covered, and my son will just get a warning." The scariest thing is that in our world, agreeing to such an offer has become the norm. And the rich father becomes a benefactor. But, in essence, this means selling your child. But if the victim is from the laborer or merchant castes, this is really the norm. At these levels, it's just a matter of selling your health.

Taya: Good afternoon. I read your comments, and essentially, something similar happened to me. Some rich kid hit me, and I sustained significant injuries. To mitigate the problem, the "roof" of that kid's family offered me to drop the charges if I signed a document. They promised to cover all the medical expenses. It sounded tempting. Initially, all the discussions with the "roof" were conducted by my parents (they are divorced) while I was in a state of shock. When I regained consciousness, I wanted to see them and discuss everything in person. I really wanted to accept their offer, but something inside me revolted, twisting at the thought that it was wrong. On the one hand, my mom urged me to accept their offer and sign the document. On the other hand, my dad was strongly against it (although he had started the conversation with them, but saw that these guys don't keep their word, so he said we couldn't trust them). I was caught between two fires, and the responsibility to make the decision lay with me. Oh, how conflicted I was for days. I was in turmoil... But I had to make a decision, so I refused their offer. A lot of dirty things were thrown at me from their side, of course. But once the decision was made and communicated, I felt relief. A wave of joy and peace washed over me. I had a clear understanding that I did the right thing.

Was this a provocation? I think it was one of the strongest ones in my life so far.

Does this mean that my refusal to accept their offer solidified my place in the warrior caste?

Klevtsova Darya: Thank you, colleague, for pointing out this aspect — who the merchant is buying his way out from. This is an essential point, and I missed it. It's acceptable to buy your way out from someone lower in the caste — a peasant. One might also try to buy their way out from an equal, from another merchant.

If a warrior allows a merchant to buy them out, accepting their terms of the game, they lose in their essence... and so does the entire warrior caste, as we know already... this, of course, is a sad situation.

Now, I understand more clearly the application of the Jewish wisdom: "If a problem can be solved with money, it's not a problem — it's an expense." You need to correctly define who you're planning to buy your way out from. At least for the simple reason that laborers and merchants will always calculate everything in terms of money. This is that simple ruse that can effectively shield you.

Fatamorgana: Since I started my education at the School, I've been regularly figuring out things that initially felt like a shock — "How can this be?" And later, I realize — yes, this world is just like that. It's better to know and use this knowledge than to live in illusions and struggle to maintain them. I've had to work hard to stop trying to save the world. Everyone is where they need to be, at the right time.

VarvaraNjord: Hello, colleagues. This is such an interesting topic and discussion. Allow me to share my thoughts. I'm actively transitioning from the merchant caste to the warrior caste, and I hope I've completed this transition. Although… it feels more like an attempt to pull me off my path, as my parents are merchants. This need to "buy my way out" has been something I've felt since childhood and hated intensely. As I read through this thread and the topic, I recalled it all so clearly... My parents, especially my mother, who was very close to me, always pursued their desires. And they pulled me into this: "Why are you sitting so sad? Let's go buy new clothes, you'll feel better!" My entire life revolved around fulfilling desires. They instilled this in me from childhood, surrounded me with it. It seeped inside me like poison. Without understanding or knowledge, I couldn't separate it from myself. But now I have. Thanks to the School. Perhaps this is my test for truly being in the warrior caste.

Previously, from every corner, I was told that if you want to develop something in the world, you need to stir up your desires, and then everything will manifest. That's the merchant slogan. It's their way of winning — quick, contractual relationships. But I was always repulsed by such relationships. I could sense, right away, that they were merchants. They'd already rushed off to the hundredth potential client. And it was painful because, no, this wasn't my like-minded person. They weren't hearing my ideas, not loyal to the order.

Merchants also caught me by pushing the level of income from a project as the measure of its growth and viability. Money is indeed considered a tool for natural selection. But for merchants, it's the only thing that matters. Yes, during the period when I fell for these slogans, I did have income. But inside, there was this feeling of wrongness. It felt unpleasant. Over time, that channel dried up because I didn't keep expanding it or reinforcing it. Selling webinars, selling and adjusting everything to sales — it's just not for me.

Thank you to all of you and the School for this knowledge. Finally, I've recognized all these attempts to pull me off course. And now I can firmly stand in the warrior caste.

Remis: If you take a close look at what's happening in the merchant caste as a whole (to understand the general trend, you need average indicators, not peaks), you will clearly see the following trend. Merchants earn money by accelerating their astral body. This is expressed in the development of two vectors: from within — their desires and the aim to fulfill them, and from the outside — by forming a multi-level network of connections (i.e., through communication). The development of these qualities is a mandatory condition for natural selection.

Ideally, by following this path, you accelerate your desires and connections so much that at some point, you simply stop understanding why you're doing all of this. You start to see that it's all just like a hamster spinning in a wheel. This is when you begin to ask yourself, "Why am I doing all of this?"

If you don't give up, don't resort to alcohol, drugs, and/or public power as an escape from internal issues, you can start working in the space of ideas and meanings, review yourself and your experiences, and continue your journey as a warrior, not a merchant.

Your mother, as you see, partially broke this algorithm + shared her current with those who didn't value it, thus diminishing the significance and value of the current itself (this is my opinion). You can assess your right to money by the merchant caste algorithm, which I've outlined above (based on my understanding).

Take a look at how you work with your astral layer of consciousness (desires + communication), and this will tell you a lot about yourself.

Andrew222: Good day, colleagues, I have a question. If someone applies for unemployment benefits, which are calculated based on the taxes they've previously paid, like in the U.S., could this affect their human rights if they seek assistance from the state? Even many merchants do this, despite their businesses and finances being in good shape. Thank you for your answer.

OksanaSidorenko: For some reason, I've always avoided government bonuses. Honestly, I'm not even aware of many of them and never specifically looked into it. For example, child benefits. My personal feeling on this matter is somewhat different from the logic. On one hand, it feels internally wrong to take money for, say, my own child. I chose to have him, what does the government have to do with it? And the bureaucratic red tape doesn't help with that feeling either. On the other hand, maybe this is exactly how people lose their rights, by refusing what is rightfully theirs. After all, everyone pays taxes... I'm not just talking about payments, but more broadly.

Zvezda: Colleagues, greetings. About government assistance... I believe it should be available. As for the laborer caste, they definitely need help without any bureaucratic barriers. Regarding merchants: if you're a successful merchant and can afford a comfortable life, you don't need to go to the state. If things are really bad, you can ask for help, it won't hurt. For warriors, it's the same, especially if the assistance is for children and you can't feed them — even if you feel that it's wrong to take aid, it's worth taking it for the children. After all, if you can have children, you should be able to provide for them, not let them starve just because you're afraid of losing some rights. Responsibility for children is crucial. But if you already have a good income and you're offered an extra 10–20 thousand, and you aim to become a mage, maybe it's best not to take it. In my opinion: as for rulers and mages, I won't comment, that's a different matter.

OksanaSidorenko: I agree with you. Of course, it's better to take care of those you are responsible for, even at the cost of losing rights, than to let them starve. The question seems to be about the appropriateness of receiving benefits outside of critical conditions. There are probably not many families in the country for whom these benefits would make a real difference.

Zvezda: Greetings, colleague. There are many families for whom such state assistance is a matter of survival. There are also many people who "have enough," but they are ready to dig the earth just to get that assistance. These are different things. If there are no critical conditions, then there's no need to take it. But if children are starving, it's important to take it, and later you can make up for it; the price will be lower than if the children (whom you've taken responsibility for) go without. It's a fine line, but we need to learn to understand and feel it if we've made a claim for something "higher."

Samorodok: In a world where no one is really responsible for anyone else anymore, this function is taken over by egregores. And the state egregore is no exception. By admitting your inability to take responsibility for your own life and the life of your children, you gain the right to receive help and care from the state.

Alexander Bandurchenko: I really like this approach in the School that a higher caste should be able to do everything that the lower castes can do. This is stated in theory in Vedic schools as well, but then they smoothly deviate from it and call school teachers brahmins because they teach. But it's clear that such brahmins wouldn't even be able to handle the level of a warrior, let alone a merchant.

Daria: I completely agree with you. I also find the approach of the School both pleasant and clear. Only by walking the path and understanding the consciousness and values of each caste can you communicate with them in their own language, guided by their values, goals (if they exist), and beliefs. Merchants are wonderful in that, when they sense something (their intuition works exceptionally well), they are open to dialogue and ready to listen. However, when laborers mask themselves as merchants, they are a wall. They will talk about themselves and their superiority, constantly seeking confirmation in the eyes of others. And out of their insecurity and fear of exposure, they will remind others of their values and goals, even though they don't actually follow them. They will deceive and steal but will always find an excuse, but if someone does the same to them, they become the enemy number one. It's a kind of "us vs. them." I find it fascinating to observe this. The light shines on the flaws they are desperately trying to hide. It could be my second nature or my passion for psychology since I was fourteen, or maybe it's all together. Since starting to study at the School in 2016, my ability to read situations and people has sharpened. I can tell what space I've entered, what values are present, what people expect, what they deny, and I have a long list of analytical questions.

When you're not a proponent of the theory of devolution, you constantly want to learn, improve your skills, and expand your consciousness. By the way, neither six months in India, nor Asia, nor Africa, nor other countries where I worked and simultaneously studied esotericism gave me real results — only the School did. I even became interested in studying chaos theory (I took risk management courses) to apply it together with practical knowledge. It's curious. You break down the situation, look at it from every angle, and... add those X and Y — who is the core of the egregore, who is involved in the situation, where the advantage lies with competitors, and what I lack, what others have, but from the perspective of elemental correlation. Then, you can form a proper analysis.

This is brief. So, the question of caste is still open. As they say, sometimes the surgeon can't perform surgery on his own eye but can direct someone else's hands... But then, the path is not magical...

Alina.Demidova: I think there are many on this forum who have been searching for themselves, understanding the world, since childhood or adolescence, and because of this, they get confused. Indeed, a laborer has no reason to think about such things, a merchant only thinks about money, and of course, the first thing that comes to mind is: "I am a warrior!" And a sense of importance follows. I have some doubts about this logical sequence.

I'm a newcomer here, just figuring things out, but I don't believe that just because you spend all your free time joyfully learning and discovering new things, that automatically means you belong to the warrior caste. It becomes especially unclear when you read comments seemingly from a warrior, but you can sense the disdain for merchants. Merchants, I understand, are seen as some sort of evil. After reading the forum, I understand that this disdain is a kind of litmus test. It seems to me that the path through castes is the path of growth. I don't believe that once you reach the warrior caste, you'll experience disdain for any other caste. After all, a warrior is someone who has been in all those roles.

The forum recommended the great movie *The Fox Hunter*, and I also found *One Breath*. There, the difference between a warrior and a merchant is very clearly portrayed. I think, as long as there are judgments of "good" and "bad," the talk about merchants and laborers doesn't matter. The fact that any free moment will be spent learning something new is no longer significant.

Nadezhda Voronina: Next, you need to earn your rights from scratch. Maybe even from minus. You'll have to fight for your place. Go up the caste ladder. It's easiest to do this when you have a dream. So, I recommend you decide to become who you want to be.

The path to this is not short. It will certainly take several years. In any case, it's better than leaving the solution to the problem for the next life. Some people, when they find themselves in such a situation, give up. But it seems that you, on the other hand, are not doing that. Learn. Apply knowledge in practice. And you will succeed.

AFTERWORD

Complete versions of the discussion of topics and questions of this book can be found on the open forum "MAGIC UNITED": wikimagic.one

In the next book, we will talk about the magical system of 12 proto-foundations; magical circles of consciousness existence; how a sorcerer differs from a mage, and much more.

Until we meet again, and I hope, very soon.

Menshikova, the School, and its students. St. Petersburg
- Minsk - Vilnius - Riga
and beyond.
2022

ADDENDUM 1
From the book by K. E. Menshikova
"Goals and Values."

THE CHANNELS
OF PHOEBUS AND DIONYSUS

The channels of Phoebus and Dionysus predetermine certain specific innate qualities that are embedded during the process of zygote[19] formation. If a person's soul, during the nine months of fetal development, is able to influence the two ancestral programs of the mother and father, selecting from the full range of qualities those that strengthen the main program (the soul), the person's nature will manifest clearly, and there will be no subsequent resistance in the consciousness. Such a person becomes self-sufficient.

However, if the soul's program is weaker than the ancestral programs, it is quite possible that the ancestral information of the mother and father will prevail—resulting in the soul occupying a secondary position in the consciousness, with a constant inner struggle guaranteed. Many of those reading this book are

---

[19] Zygote (from the Greek *zygotos* — "joined together") — a cell formed in animals and plants as a result of the fusion of male and female reproductive cells (gametes), a fertilized egg, the initial stage of embryo development.

already familiar with the theory of energy exchange and the associated psychotype[20].

A psychotype is a manifested quality, a personality trait. What we will discuss further relates to the qualities of the soul.

The development of magical consciousness always occurs within the space of myth. The tradition in which my School operates has roots in Western European thought. The myth we will discuss is the one about two fundamental forces, whose rivalry predetermines the development of human life, its evolution, and, as a consequence, the processes of cultural and civilizational growth.

Phoebus and Dionysus are names of gods from the Greco-Roman pantheon. This family of deities, like any other, existed not merely by chance, but to fulfill a specific programmatic task. The ancient Greeks worked with the proto-foundation of "Life," and everything related to humans as part of the living world also fell within the scope of their interests.

The Channel of Phoebus

Phoebus (known as Apollo in Greek mythology) is the light-bearing god, beloved by Zeus. He has many

---

[20] This topic can be studied in more detail in the book by Menshikova *"The Key to Knowing Yourself, or What is Your Uniqueness"*

names but a singular function, one that is relevant in occultism in connection with the functions of Light.

The legend tells us that Apollo was the son of the thunder god Zeus and the goddess Leto. Zeus was known for his many romantic affairs and numerous children, which makes sense considering that under his guidance, the pantheon of Greek gods worked with the proto-foundations of life, and life is always linked to creation. The goddess Leto (or Latona) is one of the oldest gods from the generation of the Titans and, according to legend, came to Hellas from the North, from the land of Hyperborea.

When Leto's time to give birth arrived, she faced great difficulties, as no earthly land was willing to provide her with a place to give birth. The reason for this was the vengeful goddess Hera, Zeus's official wife, who had cursed every land with an eternal curse, forbidding them from offering Leto a place to give birth to her children. As was often the case, Zeus distanced himself from solving the problem.

Leto wandered for a long time, burdened by the weight of the twins. Only the small island of Delos pitied her and offered her shelter, providing protection and assistance. Soon, the sunlight illuminated the island: Artemis was born first, followed by her twin brother, Apollo.

The legends of these two gods are vast, and each one holds a veiled, encoded algorithm of the victory of life and work on this channel. Apollo underwent many trials, achieving victories and defeats before finally assuming the sacred position that largely predetermined the development of civilization and crafted universal methods for achieving results on the light channel.

To look ahead, I will say that the project of creating the Institute of Egregores in its current form is entirely and completely the work of the light-bearing gods. Phoebus played no small part in this project.

After achieving several significant victories and establishing himself as a god with an incredibly large cult, Apollo became Zeus's beloved son, his right hand, and confidant. Zeus entrusted him with a very serious project: the creation of the perfect human being, made in Apollo's own image and likeness.

It is worth noting that the creation of universal living consciousness, one that would be closer to the divine, was a project pursued by all pantheons. For all of them, this was part of their technical mission, and each family of gods achieved their successes but tackled the task in different ways.

There are known projects for the creation of the "god-man" in the Semitic pantheon (Adam Kadmon), in the Egyptian pantheon (Osiris and Horus), in the Norse pantheon (the wise man Kvasir and the silent god Vidar), etc. It was believed that the pantheon of gods that created universal consciousness more quickly and effectively would rise to the top, and its religion would dominate the world. Sadly, no one has succeeded so far—neither polytheists nor monotheists.

The task of Phoebus-Apollo also focused on creating perfect consciousness. But the starting positions in the Greek pantheon were very different from those of other families of gods. Apollo needed to gather the perfect consciousness from material scattered across the entire Oikumene. This precious material had to be searched for, collected, and integrated into his channel with great care. This material—another god, the ruler of the opposite channel—was Dionysus-Zagreus.

The Channel of Dionysus (Zagreus)

The legend of this god has even more ancient roots than the legend of Apollo. We can say that Phoebus Apollo was created because Dionysus Zagreus was created before him, and the following happened to him.

First of all, we should not confuse the two gods: Dionysus Zagreus and Dionysus Bacchus. Although they are one and the same, there is still a difference. In order to understand this, let's dive into the legend, into the space of the myth about two Dionysuses.

The first Dionysus was called Zagreus, the horned god. He was born from an incestuous marriage of Zeus with his daughter Persephone. According to both branches, he is of godly origin and is originally associated with both the chthonic world of Darkness and the fiery world of Light. When he was born, Zeus exclaimed: "Behold, the Lord of All is born!" Possessing all functions of gods, all manifested and non-manifested qualities, huge as the universe and able to create any reality, Zagreus really turned out to be that unique consciousness, over the creation of which the "genetic laboratory" of Zeus had been struggling for so long. This would have been the end of the project, but that was not the case.

Zeus is a god of the third generation, not of the first one. And he had mighty relatives, the firstborn of Heaven and Earth, children of the Primordials - Gaia and Uranus - Titans. They are the lords of elemental forces, mighty earth-giants, fierce, immortal, true masters of all things. As Lucifer once did not want to worship Adam, the Titans did not recognize the power of Zagreus. The position of the Titans, as well as Lucifer's position, was simple: let him prove that he was chosen. They created a provocation by seducing little Zagreus with toys, and while he was amused, they tore him into six pieces. They consumed five of them, but Athena managed to save the sixth part - his heart. From this sixth part, Zeus created a new Dionysus later.

Having seen how they treated his best creation, Zeus in his heart burned his relatives with lightning, and the gods made men out of the dirt and ashes of Titans.

It should be said that this was not the first generation of people they had created. But every time, the result did not suit Zeus, and he destroyed the fruits of his labor: either by sea, by flood, or by fire. The generation, created from the soil and ashes of Titans, was the last one - the "race of iron" - and could not be destroyed because each living man could contain a piece of the dead Zagreus. We had to work with what we had.

People began to multiply at a rate that allowed them to arrive exponentially. The time of people flows faster than the time of gods: while Zeus breathed in and breathed out, people had time to die and be born more than once and spread over the earth like cockroaches in the kitchen of a negligent hostess. What to do? How to find in this crowd those who possess a part of universal consciousness, and how to separate them from those who are empty in this respect? This is what Phoebus Apollo, with all his ability to isolate the necessary and connect the unconnected, was needed for.

But the narrative does not end there.

Zeus places the saved part - the heart of Zagreus - in the womb of his earthly beloved, Princess Semele, who carries the new human god under her heart for six months. But vindictive Hera (where without her), having penetrated into the princess's mind, taught her how to do in such a way as to force Zeus to show his true appearance. It is known that no mortal can withstand the full power of the god's true form, and Semele was no exception. Zeus, having sworn by the waters of Styx to fulfill any wish of his beloved, was horrified when he found out what she wanted. But the waters of the Styx had a powerful effect. It was believed that the god who broke his vow had to drink water from the river of the dead and, after that, lie motionless for nine years. That is, to be out of the game. It is an obvious bid to lose, and Zeus could not afford it. He appeared before Semele in his true form, which the latter cannot withstand, and died.

Zeus removed the premature Zagreus from the womb of his dead mother, sewed him in his own hip, and carried him to term. In due time, the new Zagreus comes into the world, having received the name Dionysus - twice-born.

Half divine and half earthly in origin, Dionysus did not appear on Olympus at once. His wanderings are reflected in legends and connected with the description of madness, which his consciousness underwent until that time. Putting his legend into today's understanding, we can see that his status as Bacchus, the symbol of madness, is due to the fact that certain areas of his consciousness were created and filled with distortion.

His consciousness formed from the heart of a god but conceived with an earthly genotype predetermined that all subtle bodies, except the Mental body, would have earthly qualities. This disagreement of nature manifested itself in the discordance of consciousness and subconsciousness - they could not agree, constantly falling into conflict. This is called madness. Hence, the thirst for blood and the craving for murder manifested the presence of Dionysus in the immature minds of Bacchae, hence his wildness and cruelty, spontaneous outbursts of magic, and catastrophic lapses in memory.

Dionysus traveled the world to cure himself of madness in search of something that would allow him to realize himself. First, he was lucky to reach his grandmother, Rhea-Cybele, the mother of Zeus. Rhea, a Titaness with memory from the beginning of time, recreated the original three parts of the primary Zagreus not by the human matrix but by the divine one. She cured him of his madness by giving him *subconsciousness* and filling him with all the power of ancient knowledge. All the memory of the Earth became available to Dionysus, and he remembered himself; he remembered that he was Zagreus, the horned god. His bodies were restored: physical, Etheric, Astral, and Mental (he already had one, but it was of little use without coordination with his subconscious mind). At that moment, he has self-awareness, an awakening.

But remembering who you are, versus becoming who you are, is not the same thing.

His next step is to restore his Causal body, in order to form unified, universal algorithms of cause-and-effect relationships from comprehensive knowledge. To solve this problem, he finds Princess Ariadne, the owner of the guiding thread, having providentially made Theseus willingly refuse her. He descends to the realm of the dead and takes his mother, Semele, from there. After that, he goes up to Olympus and "*wins*" a place in the family of Olympian gods, thus officially fixing his right to participate in the common game of aspirations, which gives him the right to act as a god-creator: to form cultures and civilizations, which he began to do after leaving the divine Olympus. The movement of Dionysus goes along the northwestern trajectory, where Dionysian civilizations are created: Etruscan and Celtic civilizations in all forms.

His path is Ariadne's thread and his grandmother Rhea's instructions. She knew that to absorb infinite experience, one must gain access to the source of endless time. This source is in the hands of the god Cronus, the husband of Rhea, the god defeated by Zeus. After his defeat, Cronus resides in Elysium, the Isles of the Blessed. In Celtic mythology, it is called Avalon. A place where there is no time as a process, and there is no death either because death is a product of time. That is where Dionysus went to restore himself further.

Thus, after becoming aware of himself, Dionysus is faced with the same task as Apollo: to become complete, to form the rest of the subtle bodies, the same universal supra-consciousness as his subconsciousness became comprehensive. But how? Dionysus can act in two ways.

The first way is to continue to develop himself successively, restoring the rest of the bodies to the level of supra-consciousness.

The second way is to find parts of himself in other people and allow these parts to develop within human consciousness to the proper level, and then to unite with them as a part of himself.

Here, let us digress a little from the story of Zagreus and talk about why it is important for us.

There is such a magical law - **the Law of Contact**. It goes like this:

"Objects or beings in physical contact with each other continue to interact after separation. Everyone you have ever touched has a magical link with you, though it is probably weak unless the contact was intense and/or prolonged or repeated frequently. Magical power is contagious. Naturally, having a part of someone's body (nails, hair, spit, etc.) gives the best contagion link."

This law has found its mass application in sorcery, but it is also very important for our study: if part of a god exists in human consciousness, it will never disappear. It is just that it may be implicit or inactive up to a certain time. But once we start to wake it up, it will become stronger and stronger.

On this law and quality are built all the processes of self-awareness in magic, cognition of one's god, a part of whose consciousness gave birth to the human soul. Legends of other pantheons also tell us stories of the processes of creation of people and describe how gods separated from themselves a part of their consciousness, and this part became what in our culture is called the soul. Therefore, you can find yourself, your force, in the Greco-Roman divine family and any other pantheon. You just need to feel *your own*. The story of Phoebus and Zagreus is just a principle that was described so completely that it can be used in magic as a universal principle. That's what we are doing.

But let us get back to Dionysus.

A great secret was told to Dionysus by his grandmother Rhea. This secret allows him not only to restore himself but also to keep in touch with all the old gods who have vanished into Darkness. They are in oblivion, in Rhea's bosom, where she keeps them safe for the time being. But all informational potential of the minds of the ancient deities has not gone anywhere, and through the connection that Dionysus has found, he has gained access to the inexhaustible wealth of information. The only thing left is to gain access to the same infinite energy - time.

To fulfill this task, he went to his grandfather Cronos in Elysium. People who grow the parts of Zagreus in themselves should not be limited in resources and time. The endless time in which Dionysus resides is a resource for those who are connected with him by the principle of sympathetic connection through the parts of Zagreus that they carry in themselves.

Apollo has the same task, but he acts from the opposite side.

Firstly, he should keep Dionysus "under control" and correct his process of independent growth.

Secondly, people who are carriers of Zagreus' potential should be identified by Apollo, and their development should not be done in solitude and should follow the "correct" algorithms of light. According to the method of Phoebus, the time given to them by Dionysus should be directed not to the personal task of people but to the common task of the gods.

Both Dionysus and Apollo achieve the same thing, but their motives are quite different. The motive determines the method, and the method determines the result. Dionysus cares for himself; he must become Zagreus for his own sake. Phoebus Apollo works on Zeus' task - to create a super-intelligence in the image and likeness, to make it universal, and to be able to control both the whole process of creation and its further activity.

The motto of Dionysus: "The program must be strong and free."

The motto of Phoebus: "The program must be obedient and controllable."

The people who came through these two channels reflect these two mottos in their nature: some seek maximum freedom; others seek unlimited power.

This, of course, is a legend. A legend manifested in our mental field. But as we have found out, the fleshy mental mandala is nothing else but the imprint of multifacetedness. And now this multifacetedness is unfolding before you in volume, absorbing epochs, and times, and all manifested and unmanifested history, all spheres of human existence. Unfolding like a hologram, it manifests itself in a small way in the consciousnesses of everyone who has lived, is living, and has not yet been born; it substantiates all the processes that have been, are being, and are still being created.

People of the Phoebus Channel

The universal algorithm of victory, developed on the Phoebus channel, is as follows.

Everything on which the spot of the light channel falls becomes its property. But to build all informational components into itself consistently, it is necessary to divide the absorbed preliminary into the smallest indivisible parts. Each such part is self-sufficient, but in separation from other parts, it loses its acquired functionality and can be reprogrammed and connected with anything. In order to achieve such a result, we need a mechanism of proper separation; first of all, and secondly, the subsequent unification algorithm should work with minimal losses. That is, to make it so that all the elements that fall into the light spot and under its influence would be similar to each other, and each of them contains an element that depends on the light and is obedient to it.

This can be achieved not just by dividing objects into the smallest parts but by finding such an element in them that is necessarily present in each. That is, by the most common, the simplest quality. And this quality will be universal - uniting all elements.

One of the fundamental magical laws, **the Law of Association**, states:

"If any two patterns have elements in common, the patterns interact "through" those common elements, and control of one pattern facilitates control of the other(s) depending (among other factors) upon the number of common elements involved. This is a very important law, up there with the Law of Knowledge."

The Law of Knowledge, in turn, states: *"Understanding brings control. The more that is known about a subject, the easier it is to exercise control over it."*

The elements divided into parts lose their connection with their basis and build themselves into new organisms, into new systems. Any egregorial structure is built according to this principle, and the higher it is hierarchically, the more possibilities of separation and unification it possesses.

This is the way any light channels work. This is how the consciousness of those who are born on the Phoebus channel works.

When Phoebus traveled the world under different names, he absorbed cults and pantheons, gods and spirits, and people of different races and times.

The mechanism is simple: find what unites them and what separates them. Break each one down into small pieces, tear them from the base, destroy the divisive elements, *send them into the Darkness*, and make all the unifying elements convex, *phenomenal* for each one. Through this, a common reality will be created, a shared universe based on *one* constant, which unites all included gods, people, and spirits.

One of the magical laws, **the Law of Infinite Universes**, states:

"The total number of universes into which all possible combinations of existing phenomena could be organized is infinite."

But this is the case when the phenomenal qualities are different. But if they are the same, then the Universe becomes one single reality, acceptable to all, created in the image and likeness…

Many gods ceased to exist as part of their original maternal pantheon because they became part of a common program.

Here, it is important to see at once the difference between the algorithms of the light-bearing channel of Phoebus and seemingly similar to fiery channels of other gods, mainly of Sumer-Akkadian and Semitic origin, such as the channel of Yahweh. With all the similarities of the mechanisms, one should see the differences. The channel of Phebus and its algorithms of absorption were developed at a time when competition among different pantheons was still very strong, and therefore, it was important to fulfill one of the basic laws of development - *the principle of voluntariness*. According to this principle, any separation, absorption, and further unification could take place only upon the voluntary consent of the absorbed part.

For example, no one could dedicate a man to a god in infancy. No god, no god's cult could be absorbed without his voluntary consent. No spirit could be forced to supply the light-bearing channel with natural power unless it willed it.

The fiery channels emanating from the god Anu, from whom all monotheistic religions[21] are derived, operate in violation of this rule: the mechanism of absorption is the same, but the principle of voluntariness and personal consent is ignored. It is brought in such a form where personal consent is expressed by non-opposition, and it is considered quite sufficient.

People born on the Phoebus channel have, by nature, a unique property of seeing the main thing. In any person, phenomenon, or egregore, they unmistakably see their essence, basis, and constant - the element that allows them to be connected with other elements. They see the common; they never make a mistake in definition. That is why they have the power and, as a consequence, the right to it to a greater extent.

The task of the Phoebus channel falls upon all those who are born and work on this channel, the channel of light. It is necessary not only to create and make a universal algorithm of human consciousness development but also to ensure the introduction of this algorithm into the consciousness of those who were born on the Dionysian channel, and preferably without

---

[21] You can read more about the formation and functioning of gods and pantheons, their struggles, and results in the upcoming multi-volume series 'General Theory of Magic', as well as learn via video lessons on Menshikova's forum 'MAGIC UNITED'.

violence, on the principle of voluntary taking (or at least to create a semblance of such voluntariness). Then, all those who carry the part of Zagreus in themselves will also develop according to a "correct," predictable, controlled algorithm. This algorithm will develop only the phenomenal quality they all possess. Thus, this quality will become the constant of their consciousness, and the rest of the qualities will become variable. Sooner or later, the development will reach its extreme, when all of them will inevitably merge into a unified single mind. This will be the missing part of Dionysus Zagreus, which he simply cannot fail to take.

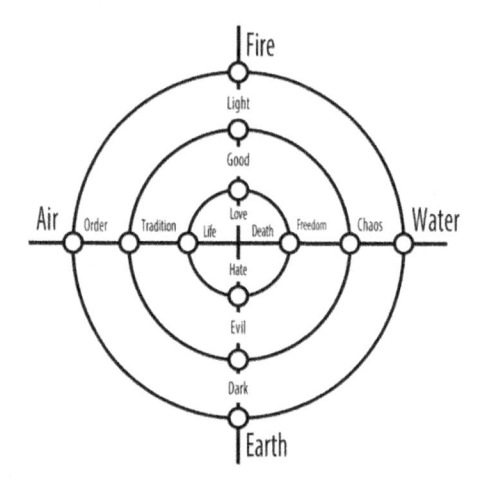

Fig. 3. Three Magic Circles Scheme

The merging of minds is possible only on the light channel. The current of light, refracting at each egregorial level, gives its effects, the main of which are the formation of the proto-foundation "Good" and the proto-foundation "Love" as its main tool.

You can see the classical scheme of reality construction and the hierarchy of informational structures. Here, there is no sense in describing the principle of action of this magical operating system, as it has no direct relation to our theme. But those who are interested in the basics of the magical construction of reality will be able to familiarize themselves with it in more detail in the series of books and lectures "The General Theory of Magic." For now, we will only touch upon those fundamentals that are inevitably activated in the consciousness when we harmonize goals and values.

The proto-foundation "Good", as you already know, contains such winning algorithms that are suitable for absolutely everyone. The effect of such acceptance is the force of love - the force of attraction.

On the channel of darkness, only separation is possible - but this is the path along which people of the Dionysus channel come. They can become self-aware only by separating themselves from the general mass, which is Evil as opposed to Good - inefficient algorithms of victory, i.e., not suitable for everyone. The tool of such separation of oneself from the mass generates the proto-foundation "Hate" - the force of repulsion.

The work of all egregors is formed on the channel of light. They gain information from the proto-foundation "Good," using its universality and richness. Egregors are the main tools of any light-bearing channel, the universal program of impact on everyone who falls into the spot of light of this or that egregore

People born on the Phoebus channel know how to do "what is right" from their earliest childhood. They don't even have to be specifically trained to do so - after some time of contemplating the reality they have been put into, they unmistakably grasp what they need to do in order not to make mistakes. And they are genuinely surprised when they see that others wish to do otherwise. This greatly annoys them, even without explanation, since their inner sense of the right algorithm for winning is very clearly manifested in them.

The Phoebus channel generously gifts leadership qualities and a thirst for power to its conduits. Power **is one of the most important values** for those born on this channel. Pay attention to this. Phoebus has a natural need to spread his influence over a large number of people. He has no interest in gaining influence through the cheap popularity of spontaneous egregors for a brief moment. Phoebus needs to get the right to direct the endless current of time in the desired direction for a long time, forever.

The qualities of power are manifested in the people of the Phoebus channel literally from the cradle. As soon as the first steps of self-awareness and self-identification are taken, they begin to manifest the rules of their own understanding of order.

Phoebus is not curious. Not at all. Because he has no need to explore the reality around him. The task of this channel is to create the rules for the existence of an ideal reality, to bring into the world an idea that everyone will accept, and to absorb all the realities it can reach.

The big problem of people of the Phoebus channel is that some of them are not good at separating things into parts. They can hardly separate the necessary thing from the unnecessary one. The consciousness of intellectually poor Phoebus contains ideas of globalism, which, on a primitive level, is expressed in denial of the whole if the part is undesirable. Mentally developed people of the Phoebus channel know how to separate the main from the secondary, and through this quality, they are more effective in absorbing.

If Phoebus correctly understands his nature and does not deny it, he initially enters a favorable environment, which allows him to be fairly successful. He is the favorite of different egregorial structures that gladly make him their conduit. On his path, Phoebus always meets those who offer him their help voluntarily.

Even without knowing the laws of magic concerning balance and voluntariness, they intuitively feel that these laws are important, and it is better not to violate them. Therefore, as a tool, they develop methods of psychological impact and learn to work competently with the word and the principle of law. Their task is to make Dionysus get into the light spot and voluntarily stay in it. Dionysus should sincerely like the idea, the principle of life, and the rule of coexistence so that he would want to absorb the algorithm for constructing consciousness developed by Phoebus.

The Phoebus channel will not deal with the question: is there a part of Zagreus in the consciousness that it absorbs, or is there no part of it and never was? If there is, it will definitely manifest itself sooner or later on the light current, and if there is no - the consciousness will be absorbed and will become food for the channel together with time. Suppose one is able to absorb a critical amount of Zagreus' parts, reprogram them with the right algorithm, and *unite them into a network*. In that case, all the others who have not been absorbed yet will definitely feel it and become more receptive to the universal algorithm - this is what Phoebus thinks; this is what the light channel thinks. This is how people born on this channel think and act.

People born on the Phoebus channel will try to spread their values to everyone, at least within the egregorial layer, which is under their control, whether it is their family, spontaneous formation, profession, or state. But they have many more opportunities in religion. Their confidence in their own rightness and the sense of their own power opens all doors and give them a lot of opportunities.

The task of the Phoebus channel becomes clear: to spread its light spot as widely as possible, to make it all-encompassing (at least outwardly) for all those who enter it. Thus, those who are included in the light of Phoebus are assured that the same thing happens everywhere. Phoebus, in general, is a master of illusions and adherents of erasing boundaries.

The people of the Phoebus channel are rarely wrong, so for the most part, their rightness is always appropriate, predominantly for the same Phoebus, but also for those Dionysus who have not yet recognized and felt his nature and have not had much experience in this life.

…The human nature of Phoebus: he cannot but care for those around him. Starting from the family level to the state and religious level, he doesn't do anything in life for himself. If his care (read - power) is not claimed by anyone, this makes him unhappy and shows his functional inferiority.

Care for Phoebus is power. It is manifested through the security indicator. The one who voluntarily accepts his care automatically accepts his power over oneself - such is the algorithm.

The law is sacred to the Phoebus people. Roman civilization is the purest product of the deed of Phoebus. That is where Roman law and all the rules and Roman law that all state egregorial entities still rely on came from. That is where all the rules and Roman Law came from, which all state egregorial formations still rely on today. Dura lex, sed lex - the law is harsh, but it is the law. That is where the rule of Phoebus, which still works, was approved: "What is not on paper is not in nature." That is, what is not manifested in the level of the Mental body, what is not in the spot of light, simply does not exist.

Literate and educated Phoebus are very fond of the law. And Latin. Even if they do not know anything about magic, it does not prevent them from feeling that every time they use a winged Latin phrase, it is as if they have an additional source of inner strength, and the state of unshakable rightness becomes stronger and stronger. This happens because, through these key phrases, they can connect with their primary source, with the holder of the principle of light - Phoebus Apollo himself.

There is even a corresponding magical **Law of Words of Power**, which states:

"There exist certain words that are able to alter the internal and external realities of those uttering them, and the power may rest in the very sounds of the words as much as their meanings. Many of such words are names, though the meanings may have been lost or forgotten. Many magical tools require words to be inscribed upon them and/or said over them during their construction and/or use."

It is echoed by **the Law of the Names**:

"Knowing the complete and true name of an object, being, or process gives one complete control over it. This works because a name is a definition as well as a contagion link, and an association (if you call something the same name over and over, that name becomes associated with the thing). This also works, because knowing the complete and true name of something or someone

means that you have achieved a complete understanding of it's or their nature."

These two laws predetermine that the Phoebus channel (and the people born on it) will develop their abilities and power in the mental realm, affecting the goals of others and subjugating them to their value. You have already seen the effect of this in your studies. The method consists of the possession of speech and the gift of persuasion. If you call a table a chair for a long time and convince others to do the same, after a while, the table will become a chair. If you call good benefit and evil harm, and everyone you extend your influence on will do the same, then such definitions will appear in the general mental realm. If death is regarded as evil and life as good, then after a while, everyone else will start to think the same way without thinking why.

The word is Phoebus' strongest weapon. That is why Phoebus has maximum effect when he opens his mouth and starts to say something. At this moment, the full force of Apollonian natural power is able to awaken in him, and the connection with the light channel of the progenitor becomes stronger and more powerful, which is completely different from the state when Phoebus is silent or refuses to apply his gift to the surrounding reality.

Hence, the advice to those who, within the framework of this work, will uniquely define themselves as Phoebus: learn to use the power of the word. In addition, learn Latin and use it more often (remembering the Law of Words of Power). It is not without reason that before Reformation, all clergymen and representatives of the highest spiritual nobility communicated only in Latin, even among themselves, and were obliged to know this language better than their native. Maybe this language is "dead" nowadays, but it was a very working one in the past.

The people of the Phoebus channel should study a lot and be very educated. This will help them to use with greater efficiency all the power of the channel, given to them by birthright, and also will instill a mandatory skill of success on this channel - the ability to separate any event/appearance/thing to the smallest parts and not to slip into globalism and religious obscurantism.

People of this channel make not only excellent leaders and rulers but also priests - conduits of forces and cult workers. They sensitively feel the scheme of the ritual and never allow themselves to improvise. They know how to feel the rate of energy during the rite, how to breathe in rhythm with it, and how to *incorporate the right words into this rhythm*.

Such priestly potency among people of the Phoebus channel extends not only to religion and service but also to society: they can perfectly set the pace of life for everyone else, manage time, and direct it in the right rhythm in the right direction. This gift was bestowed upon them by the lord of the channel, Phoebus Apollo, predetermining that only with such ability it is possible to take and hold power. Indeed, the majority of people do not understand how to *spend* their time and will gladly give it to someone who knows how and can demonstrate their knowledge only through the right and timely spoken word.

As true priests in magic, the people of the Phoebus channel will never change the channel and, with all the wealth of choices, will always try to stay committed to their force. The magical **Law of Pragmatism,** which in this capacity will always support them, states:

"If a pattern of belief or behavior enables a being to survive and to accomplish chosen goals, then that belief or behavior is "true" or "real" or "sensible." If it works, it's true."

This rule is sometimes shunned, but ... it's usually applied.

From Phoebus's point of view, any lie is justified by the task at hand.

All the more so because the natural passion for globalism will always give Phoebus the understanding that the result and the obtained effect *will spread to everyone and make his spot of light a safe space for those who get into it, and for this, all means are good.*

If Phoebus's goals do not support the value of "safety for others" but instead try to show only personal interest, be sure - they will be realized in the very last turn.

The people of the Phoebus Channel depend on constants. This is their nature: constants are unbreakable, and constants will always exist. It is only important to find a universal constant, a *fundamental law* that will apply to everyone, like gravity. As long as Phoebus is in search of his constants, he is like Dionysus and will never be successful in this capacity. But as soon as he establishes himself in the most important value, makes it visible or tangible, and sees how it gives "calmness" to all those around him, he gets runaway success. In magic, this quality is also expressed by **the Law of Cause and Effect**:

"If exactly the actions are done under exactly the same conditions, they will be associated with exactly the same results. The key to magical success is learning which variables are the most important, and how to keep them constant."

People of the Dionysus Channel

Titans, having killed the first Dionysus Zagreus, wanted him to go through all the proper stages of self-growth to collect his missing parts himself. If he succeeds in this search for himself and restores his own essence, he will be rightfully called the Lord of All.

Moreover, the power of the elements, naturally present in Titans, has also been given to the new Dionysus - it is a gift of the primordial, natural forces. Not only the scattered parts of Zagreus's mind but also the elemental magical components constitute the wealth of those who are born on this channel. All this is the starting capital for the coming creation of oneself:

informational particles of God and potential magical power.

People of the Dionysus channel carry his potential within themselves. The inner resistance of their nature does not allow them to take light algorithms of connection with reality willingly. If circumstances and the environment still force them to agree, the inner conflict in these cases only grows.

The nature of Dionysus cannot allow them to collect themselves according to Phoebus's algorithm - this is the risk of losing oneself, losing one's identity, and killing one's purpose. He needs to take the maximum of experience, all experience, even if it is ineffective from the point of view of the egregorial environment.

The Dionysus channel moves its people in the process of natural development from bottom to top, starting from the energetic bodies, integrating it with the mental, and further on to the independent, individual development of supra-consciousness. As a result, the human being must reach his true values, *find his god, and unite with him*, never being satisfied with the proposed variants coming from the channel of Phoebus: **not my god who is worshiped by all, but the one who is the essence of me.**

In contrast to the channel of light, the dark channel inspired by Dionysus denies ideals. Its main credo is that universality can only be achieved by collecting all the experiences that exist in the world. This means that the mind should not have long-term preferences; superficial motives change if they are learned; goals are forgotten if they are achieved. No single experience can be universal enough to absorb other experiences - they will always differ in some way, and this difference is also a subject for investigation and, thus, a reason for new experiences.

Any experience is important, including mistakes (they are, to a greater extent). You need to go through all the mistakes and find the right use for each one. That is, to form your own unique algorithms of goodness, which will never 100% repeat other algorithms.

One of the laws of magic, **the Law of Personal Universe**, which supports the channel Dionysus, says this:

"Every sentient being lives in and quite possibly creates a unique universe which can never be 100% identical to that lived in by another. So called "reality" is in fact a matter of consensus opinions."

The peculiarity of the consciousness of those who have accepted their Dionysian nature is that it is never satisfied with the achieved and disrespects authority. They spend their whole life inventing the wheel, not because they are unfamiliar with its device, but in order to understand how it works.

If Phoebus was recommended to use Latin more often, then Dionysus, on the contrary, is recommended to avoid it in order not to connect even accidentally with the current of light of Phoebus, especially if the consciousness is not ready for such an examination.

Because any systematization of consciousness, any stereotyping of thinking, any templating will force Dionysus to suppress his nature, to neglect the original properties of nature.

...The human nature of Dionysus requires cognition, taking all the experience that is possible in this egregorial field. And if the egregore can no longer offer Dionysus anything new, it will be replaced very quickly, regardless of any obligations and laws.

The commandment that Dionysus Zagreus left to his followers: time should be spent on gaining experience. That's what the channel was built for. The channel of time, the channel of knowledge hidden in the darkness. The channel that unlocks the proto-foundation "Evil" for those born on it - everything that was rejected by the Phoebus channel as unnecessary, not fitting the safety standards, must be taken by Dionysus and get a second chance, a second birth. Only people of the Dionysian channel can do such a thing. From the point of view of the Phoebus, they are embodied evil, carriers of qualities that are unnecessary in the world. Unnecessary as not having passed the selection for uniformity, for suitability for all.

It is this initial consciousness programming that makes Dionysus to be a personality sometimes insufferable to surrounding people. And the more vividly the parts of Zagreus are manifested, the more unconventional character they have from birth. Unfortunately, not everyone is able to maintain this quality in the endless current of light; not everyone hardens like a Sumerian clay tablet in the sun - many melt like wax with ancient Etruscan writings.

Any experience that Dionysus receives becomes his personal property. Any experience he takes "on faith" makes it the property of the channel of Phoebus.

Dionysus must dismantle his mental constructions every day, and before going to bed, he must break them up in order to repeat the process in the morning based on new knowledge and new personal experiences of the previous day. He begins to lose as soon as he is satisfied with the obtained result and leaves his mentality static.

People whose consciousness is able to work on the dark channel of Dionysus, people born on it, are very curious. Everything is interesting to them, and there is nothing that could seem ordinary; even well-known things are revealed in such a consciousness each time differently.

Dionysuses never settle down on one method of realizing their tasks. They do not seek any power; their main motive is interest. Only fear of darkness, of the unknown, can keep them from changing life.

Dionysus should not think about safety - neither his own nor that of others. If his values begin to be dominated by security, and only his own and not that of others, he becomes very limited Dionysus, almost killed by the system. Dionysus, who has not been cured by Rhea and does not know the power of his subconsciousness, will be scared to the knees about it. If such a Dionysus begins to take precedence over his interest, then he is a dead person, a dead Dionysus. He is not able to use the power of the time channel, the power of Rhea, and time becomes inaccessible to him, which means certain death. And this is not a figure of speech - not only mental death but also physical, quite real.

The best way to deactivate Dionysus is not just to absorb him into the spot of light of the Phoebus channel but also to frighten him with darkness, to make him never come close to what is forbidden, to what in the egregorial light world has to do with evil. Taking into account the fact that both darkness and evil (not in the egregorial, but already in the magical sense) are the nature of Dionysus, with such beliefs in his consciousness, he will never look deep into himself. Scared of himself, afraid of himself, he contributes his consciousness and time to someone who doesn't do that, who dissolves it in himself and gives Dionysus the illusion of security, the illusion of the achieved result.

In magic, Dionysus will never succeed in ritualism - it is difficult for them to follow the sequence of actions. Therefore, Dionysus will never become a good priest. Yes, he can be a sorcerer or warlock, but his nature is not capable of holding the channel by repeated repetitions of the same thing, neither physically nor mentally. He is interested in many things, and he can never *be faithful* in the classical sense of the term.

Just as it is true that Phoebus would rather live according to the Law of Pragmatism, so it is also true that **the Law of True Falsehoods** applies to Dionysus:

"It is possible for a concept or act to violate the truth patterns of a given personal universe and still be "true", provided that it "works" in a specific situation. If it's a paradox, it's still probably true."

Dionysus seeks himself everywhere and is ready to change channels of different gods like gloves in order to find himself. The concept of "faithfulness" does not apply well to Dionysus. In the same way, they go through people, events, things, and phenomena... All with the sole purpose of not repeating themselves.

Dionysus may stop loving another person if he recognizes that the object of his love has sympathy for someone else. And his love won't become cold but will be over. And it is not even the lack of desire to compete, but a deep conviction: if this person (thing, phenomenon) is needed for someone else, then either the phenomenon is not unique, or I am. Both are unacceptable to the consciousness of Dionysus: one's own uniqueness must always come first, which means that events, phenomena, and people present "here and now" must also possess this quality - otherwise, he will get rid of them.

Phoebus, in such a situation, on the contrary, will fight "for what belongs to him" to the end. Whether or not it is necessary, he will figure it out later, but the clear conviction that *he cannot give away "something that belongs to him"* runs through his entire consciousness. In this case, the concept of "something" also applies to people, relationships, and memory - everything that his mind once called "mine".

The value of time is very well manifested in the consciousness of Phoebus. Not having by nature, the right to unlimited time, they know how to value it. People of the Dionysus channel, on the contrary, bathe in this source and have no value of time. They can spend it unnecessarily on some nonsense: the feeling of an endless source creates an illusory idea that it will always be so. Dionysus thinks that he will live forever, so he doesn't manage to do much in life.

If a child is born on the Dionysian channel, but both his parents are Phoebuses, then we can say that he was trapped in the cruelest karmic conditions: he not only needs to develop himself, fulfilling his purpose in life but also to learn to defend his own interests in this fiercest struggle. Such conditions are a sort of injection. If he withstands the primary karmic circumstances, he will become truly resilient for his whole life. After all, if he has managed to preserve himself in love, it will be much easier to do so in hate.

If a child Phoebus is born into the Dionysian family, he will face the same test: the family, as a test environment, must develop primary skills of controlling those who are older and more important, but by nature, Phoebus is obliged to obey. If he manages to overcome this cognitive dissonance, the road to power and the support of light will be guaranteed for him in the future.

Remember that parents are not enemies. That is just a test shell, which gives an opportunity to hone the skills of interaction with the big world in a state of relative physical safety.

People of the Phoebus channel and the Dionysus channel are natural antagonists. But they cannot exist without each other. To whom will people of the Phoebus channel apply universal algorithms of power? Against whom will people of the Dionysus channel fight, honing their competitiveness? Who needs light if there is no darkness? Who needs darkness if there is no opportunity to manifest it? Their confrontation is expressed in an endless struggle with each other: Dionysus runs away, Phoebus catches up, Phoebus creates egregors, Dionysus invents mechanisms to escape them; Phoebus is a programmer, and Dionysus is a hacker. The purpose of such confrontation is not so much the result as the constant development of mechanisms "how?" How to make a program that no Dionysus can escape? How to develop such qualities of consciousness that will allow one to escape any light-bearing program?

Only at first sight does this confrontation take the form of enmity. Phoebus and Dionysus are not enemies of each other; they are brothers but rivals. That's the way nature made them. It sets the rhythm of life for all people who carry in themselves the potential of immortal brothers.

Phoebus becomes smarter in this confrontation, more cunning and insightful. Dionysus develops intuition, learns to use his subconscious to its full potential, awakens the Dionysian magic in himself, and becomes stronger in the process of natural selection.

Phoebus will give neither power nor time to his rivals - he simply doesn't have them. But he will provide information, give universal algorithms of victory, and teach them how to add time to their life. Dionysus will not teach the bearers of his potential how to win; universal algorithms of success are unknown to him. But he will give his people infinite power and endless time. Of course, if they manage to take it.

Dionysus does not single out anyone personally - whoever succeeded is the best. Phoebus leads his people from the beginning up to the end.

The conflict between the two channels is systemic and inspired by the fundamental law of evolution - development and growth. Through their qualities and this conflict, Phoebuses build civilization, and Dionysuses develop culture.

Culture grows on the grapevine of Dionysus, but the owner of this vineyard is Apollo.

Dionysus is the pioneer. Wherever he went, local culture flourished. But Phoebus followed behind and built the created into the structure of the law. Dionysus created cults, and Phoebus made religion out of cults. They followed each other through the forest, and along the mountains of Europe, and where their way past, the most powerful civilizations were formed, on the strength of which mankind exists to this day: Roman, Gallic, Celtic, and British.

If it is true that Dionysus is a tree, it is just as true that Phoebus is a gardener.

Only your values will show you who you are - look at them. Don't listen to your Mental body; it will deceive you. Now, it is carefully selecting arguments for and against, trying to pick out from the whole volume of information one that corresponds to its habitual self-understanding. Now, it is lying for quite understandable reasons: the picture of the world falling apart along with the illusory view of your own life. Look only at your values and answer honestly what your nature is.

If you think you are somebody who you are not, you will destroy yourself. Embrace your nature. It will explain a lot and give a lot.

People who have defined themselves as being born on the Phoebus channel should ask themselves again:

1. Can I live without power? Am I willing to obey without subsequently exerting my will on other people?
2. Am I willing to sacrifice my interest for the safety of those who trust me?

People born on the channel of Dionysus should ask themselves:

1. Am I able to sacrifice interest for stability?

2. Am I willing to obey the rules and get satisfaction from it?

If we look at the presence of Phoebus people and Dionysian people in our world in terms of percentage, we can easily see that there are slightly more people born under the Dionysian channel. Ideally, the proportions of both should revolve around the golden ratio: 62% of people from the Dionysian channel and 38% from the Phoebus channel. But this is the ideal, and in reality, it is somewhat different. Furthermore, on each land, this proportion will be unique, but overall, in relation to a relatively distinct structure (such as all of humanity, one independent race, one religion, etc.), the "golden proportion" should be maintained.

If there are more people of Dionysian nature, chaos increases; if there are more Phoebus people than necessary, the system starts to become excessively ordered, entropy grows, and development slows down. Nature itself regulates this process by strengthening one channel and diminishing the other.

From the book by K. E. Menshikova
"Goals and Values."

GEIS

The Irish Celtic tradition developed within itself the methods of achieving and maintaining ideal power. Irish Celtic civilization is a project aimed at developing the consciousness of the ideal ruler. The entire focus of this tradition was to develop universal methods of behavior, thought, and action for those worthy of royal power. Those who can take responsibility for themselves and get real results in the process, those who can be responsible not only for themselves but also for others.

According to the ancient law, it is not the people who choose the king. The king is chosen by the Earth, its personified mind expressed in the image of the goddess. In Ireland she was called Eriu, Erin[22] and had

---

[22] The sagas tell us that when the Sons of Míl conquered Ireland, they met Banba and Fodla, each one of them asked for an island to be named after her. When they reached Usnech, the central part of the country, they met a third goddess, Eriu, who addressed the Sons of Míl with the same words. These were the three faces of one goddess, and thrice the Sons of Míl made this promise.

The Sons of Míl were a tribe of men, replacing the gods, the sons of the goddess Danu. The threefold oath was the basis of the alliance between Earth and men. Since then, the man became the husband to the Earth, the True King and ruler, and the ancient gods yielded

three faces. The one who receives the right to power from the goddess must be flawless, so the ancients believed. The principle of impeccability for gaining power in the Irish Celtic civilization was developed to perfection.

Only a ruler who had at least three generations of impeccable ancestors in his lineage could be considered a true king. He must always be true to his word, always pay his debts. Moreover, it was believed that physical imperfection was a clear indicator of a secret vice, a violation of the principle of impeccability[23].

The Druids gave those on the path of self-improvement specific tasks in order to hone certain important phenomenal qualities that would later form the basis of the general principle of impeccability. They were always associated with fulfillment of certain

---

their place to him - that was the choice of the goddess. So, the ancient legend tells us.

[23] A physical vice, according to the ancients, could only manifest itself as a consequence of sorcery, and sorcery would only affect a person if the fili (mage) sings a "blasphemous song" or "song of reproach" (glam dicenn) on that person. At the same time, it was believed that a fili would never do this simply on the basis of personal preference: the mage sees what is hidden from everyone, he sees the secret vulnerability of the king and makes it appear now so that everyone sees the Ruler's imperfections. Usually in such cases, the king was deposed and replaced by a more flawless consciousness. In contrast, the "song of praise" worked like a blessing - it raised the EV of the ruler, making his consciousness even more phenomenal from the position of impeccability.

obligations: to do something or not to do something under certain circumstances. That's what geis is.

To impose geis is to weave a metal thread into the fabric of fate, which will become a guiding thread through all stages of life; it will not let you lose your way and will always remind you of who you are.

The inclusion of consciousness in the geis system is very important for someone who follows the warrior path of self-development, who takes his life into his own hands and tries to become as independent as possible from circumstances, from the system and from the weaknesses of others. In the Slavic tradition, the institution of geis also existed, but we know them under different names: vow, promise, oath.

A geis could be placed by a druid (fili) on a king or other person but could also be taken on its own. The latter was usually done by those who did not belong to the royal bloodline but aspired to reach heights not determined by birth, not determined by fate.

For the king, the placed geis was not just an obligation. The king knew and had no doubt that not only his own fate, but also the fate of the whole country, his people, depended on his observance of the rules of impeccability, on his adherence to his geis. The druid who placed the geis never expressed his personal will: the seer, talking to the gods, heard their instructions and transmitted what he heard to the ruler, putting it in the form of an action understandable for him, the ruler.

Druids are the conduits of magic in this world, those who keep the balance and control the correct execution of magical tasks. One of the most important functions of the druids' activity was to recognize and assign key figures without error, to see constants and make them stronger, more significant, implementing the law *of cause and effect* already known to you.

The burden a druid imposed on a person was never idle and meaningless - it always implied long-range plans even if they were not apparent at first glance, and the action-game seemed absurd. But many years of performing geis not only developed in the ruler the qualities of character necessary for impeccability but also made him a knot in the fabric of reality with which it was impossible not to reckon: under certain circumstances a certain action will always be performed, and there can be no variability and randomness at this point in space-time. This means that *the gods can rely on him.*

Unlike a ruler who cannot choose his own geis, a warrior has this right. A ruler is a protégé of the higher powers, a conduit of their will. He is given a lot but for this the degree of his freedom is diminished. The warrior does not have the same resources as the ruler, but in contrast, has a greater degree of freedom. Including the independent choice of geis.

On what basis should a warrior impose a geis on himself? Based on recognizing his own imperfection, his own flaws. It's all the things that can make him vulnerable at any moment. It's what makes him accept defeat without even trying to fight. Do you have that quality? It is always present in those who live in the human world. It is impossible to dismiss it, to turn a blind eye to the presence of vice in one's consciousness. You should fight it. Fight and win.

To do this, one must apply the principle of placing a geis *onto oneself* - to do as the free warriors of old times did when they wanted to overcome their imperfection and become what they were not - having the right, having power over themselves.

For each identified flaw, one should take a vow, place a geis on oneself - perform a *regular* action that will slowly but surely eradicate this quality from the consciousness, diminish it in order to make room for the algorithms of victory - the kind of victory that develops the nature, goes in unison with nature, not contradicts it.

What's stopping you from achieving results? Laziness? So, it should be actions that will banish this quality. Consciously perform *regular* actions that will go against the weaknesses of the subconscious, despise laziness: running in the morning, learning a language for an hour a day, dousing yourself with cold water - doing exactly what you do not like, what causes irritation and activates the first contour of subconscious defense.

What else? Ignorance? So, not only do you need to take regular actions that will make you an educated person, but just as importantly, you need to eradicate the sense of pride and satisfaction in your own ignorance, to remove from your consciousness the sense of rightness from believing but not knowing. Do not take anything on faith, check every piece of information, no matter who it comes from, and do not rest until you understand it completely. Such a task requires a specific action: don't go to bed until you have done it; don't eat until you have learned it - the stricter the restrictions, the faster the result.

Cowardice? Take a geis related to overcoming fear: skydiving, walking in the evening in the dark and always a different road, initiating a conversation.

Shyness, inability to stand up for yourself? This is also a type of cowardice - fear of people. Here is the counteraction that can help to get rid of this quality - to meet a new person every day; do not spare time and effort making sure that the person himself wants to tell you his life. And the main thing is not to be afraid of looking funny, not to be afraid of losing face.

And so, for every vice, for every flaw take not an abstract but a very real action, developing the will and inner nature.

* * *

Magical transformation of consciousness begins to occur when the existential volume rises to such a level that it becomes phenomenal — distinct from the consciousness of the general human mass. From this moment, all transformations and increases in possibilities will progress geometrically — you just need to prove your resilience, pass all provocations, and convince your natural force that you have the right to be who you want to be and are ready to match the declared status.

* * *

The magical tradition in which my School operates is based on an ancient system of pagan magic. Its roots go back to the northern tradition as well as the old Druidic school. Unlike today's religions, the old gods demanded from their human conduits not so much correct thinking as correct actions. It is not enough, they taught, to repent after committing an abomination and then do nothing. One must take real actions to counter the wrong ones. It is not enough to just think correctly; there must necessarily be an action that follows the thought, which allows one to take rather than wait for what is given by divine grace. The old tradition nurtured and educated a generation of warriors, a generation of those who must lead others and protect those who cannot yet do so themselves.

In the manifested reality, the ancients taught, in the world of first attention, a warrior must leave behind such traces that show you did not waste your time — this is on one hand. On the other hand, the traces left by a warrior must be so significant that their presence must inevitably be reflected in the lives of all subsequent generations — they simply cannot ignore it. The greater the period of time over which such a trace spreads its influence, the more substantial the consciousness of the one who left that trace becomes.

Therefore, the duration for which a geis is taken depends on the scale of the task before you. If it involves a total change of fate, acquiring rights that neither you nor your ancestors ever had, then the geis is taken for life. If it is about "short-term" acquisitions or the development of a specific skill, the term of the geis may be finite. In our tradition, this term is usually annual: from Samhain to Samhain.

And you will succeed.

Made in United States
Orlando, FL
24 February 2025